Whop Biscuits & Fried Apple Pie

Cooking with Gatlinburg's Great Smoky Arts & Crafts Community

Kathy Shields Guttman

WsV

Wordsmith Ventures
Toronto, Canada

Published by Wordsmith Ventures, 6021 Yonge Street, Suite 300, Toronto, Ontario M2M 3W2.

Canadian Cataloguing in Publication Data
Guttman, Kathy Shields, 1948–
    Whop biscuits & fried apple pie : cooking with Gatlinburg's Great Smoky arts & crafts community
Includes index.
ISBN 0-9681144-0-7
1. Cookery - Tennessee - Gatlinburg. 2. Cookery, American - Southern style. 3. Artists - Tennessee - Gatlinburg - Anecdotes. 4. Artisans - Tennessee - Gatlinburg - Anecdotes. I. Title. II. Title: Whop biscuits and fried apple pie.
TX715.2.S68G87 1996   641.59768'893   C96-931871-5

Cover illustration and interior art work by Betty Jane Posey
Book design and composition by Ian MacKenzie, ParaGraphics, Toronto
Production services by Gwenne Becker of Becker Associates, Toronto
GSACC logo used with permission

Printed in Canada

Dedication

This book is dedicated to my mother, Ruth Simmons Shields, and to the memory of my father, Martin (Bert) Shields.

Acknowledgments

A heartfelt thanks goes to all those members of the Great Smoky Arts & Crafts Community who shared their recipes with me, as well as special memories, favorite places, and practical hints and tips. Getting to know you was the best part of compiling this book. Being warmly greeted as the "Cookbook Lady" was something I looked forward to each time I opened your studio doors. It has been an experience I will treasure for a lifetime. Special thanks to Susan McDonell (at the start of this project she was the GSACC president) for inviting me to one of their meetings to introduce the cookbook idea to the members and for conveying her enthusiastic support. Also thanks to the current president of the GSACC, Buie Boling, for her continued support and help. A special note of thanks to Betty Jane and Cecil Posey, without whose help, support, and encouragement this book may never have been a reality. I could not have asked for two better cheerleaders. Another cheerleader I must thank is my friend Frieda. "Just do it!" was her constant advice. Her help in keeping me focused on this project and constructive comments, as well as editorial assistance was invaluable. To my best buddy, and official taste-tester, Rosemarie, I thank you for your support and friendship. To Gwenne Becker and Ian MacKenzie thanks for your assistance, guidance, and patience in working with a complete novice. And last, but not least, thanks to my family. My two daughters, Katana and Ariela, have been great sports through all the feast and famine I have put them through these last few years; from the many dishes you taste-tested (even trying foods you do not like), to the times you had to fend for yourself when I was too busy to cook. To the newest members of our family, Launy and Annissa, thanks for not complaining about all the frozen dinners and fast food while I finished the writing of this book. To Hershel, my husband, my best friend, and number one supporter, I thank you for your love, patience, business sense, common sense, and sense of humor . . . now, if only you would learn to pronounce *apricot* correctly, you'd be perfect!

Contents

Finding Gatlinburg

Introduction

"Why is someone from Toronto, Canada writing a cookbook with recipes from artisans in Gatlinburg, Tennessee?" I must have been asked that question about a hundred times in the last few years. The short answer is I fell in love with the Smoky Mountains, its regional food, and its arts and crafts community. I wanted to find a way to share my discovery with others.

The long answer is not as easy to explain. While on a planned vacation to Tennessee and Kentucky, my husband and I decided to drop in for one night to check out Gatlinburg and The Great Smoky Mountain National Park. We never made it to our other destinations. Each day we would extend our stay for another day, until our vacation was over.

In the morning we would awake to see a blue mist surrounding the mountains. On our hikes and drives we discovered lazy rivers and rushing waters. We sat on huge boulders enjoying a picnic lunch alongside cascading waterfalls.

In the local restaurants we delighted in good old-fashioned southern cooking and hospitality. We sampled our first grits at breakfast, served with hot biscuits and butter topped with sorghum molasses and blackberry preserves. We lunched on steaming hot bowls of homemade soups and scrumptious sandwiches, big bowls of spicy chili, and tender corn bread.

For dinner we ate fresh trout and catfish, barbecue pork and southern fried chicken, boiled cabbage, country green beans, and corn bread salad. Southern specialties such as pecan pies, peach cobblers, fried apple pies, and stack cakes were some of the irresistible offerings on the dessert menu.

One morning while my husband was out on a climb up the Chimney Tops peak, I drove off to explore the region. In a little valley three miles outside of downtown Gatlinburg, I discovered an incredible community of artists and craftspeople. They were the "icing on the cake" to what was already a wonderful vacation.

It was on our second trip to the Smokies, while chatting with the artisans and asking them about the best places in town to eat, that I first got the idea for this cookbook. Some of the artisans would go into great detail describing the delicious trout, the tastiest hushpuppies, the largest buffets, and the best homemade pies. As I listened, I felt the seeds of a cookbook idea starting to sprout. After all, cooking is a form of art. And it stands to reason if cooking and creativity go hand-in-hand, and artists are naturally creative, then the perfect ingredients for a good cookbook would be artists sharing their favorite recipes. It all added up: cooking, creativity, artists.

Our conversations graduated from restaurants to how they prepare their own favorite foods: slowly simmering a sauce for spaghetti, cooking corn-on-the-cob on a campfire, or how the trick to good biscuits is not to "dough" it too much. The next thing I knew, they were telling me who had a great recipe for pound cake, how the deli down the street makes a great sandwich, and how the wife of a woodcarver had people drive in all the way from Atlanta to buy her fried apple pies at the church fundraiser. After listening a little longer, I knew that these artisans would be the best people to tell you about the Smokies—its food, its art, and its special places.

Now you know why a "foodie fanatic" from Canada is writing a cookbook with recipes from Tennessee. As you read the recipes and turn the pages of this book, you will meet artisans who are Gatlinburg natives; their families having lived in the Smokies for generations. Others have various southern roots and accents. There are northerners and those who hail from America's heartland. There is even a New Englander and a former Canadian.

By sharing with you their recipes and stories (and those of some of their family and friends), I hope to give you a taste of the group's diversity: their art, their personalities, and their skill and creativity in the kitchen. The hints and tips, quotes and anecdotes, references to special places, and reflections on life as an artist I hope will spice up your reading enjoyment and let you experience, through the artisans own words, the uniqueness of Gatlinburg and the Great Smoky Arts & Crafts Community.

Great Smoky Arts & Crafts Community
Historical Perspective

No place in North America is more synonymous with handcrafts and fine art than Gatlinburg, Tennessee. While the rest of America was involved in an industrial revolution in the late nineteenth and early twentieth centuries, the farmers of Gatlinburg were doing what they had always been doing. Since they settled their valley in the 1790's: they had grown, shot, and trapped their own food; built their own shelters; brewed their own whiskey; and made everything they needed to survive and enhance the quality of their lives.

In 1912 the teachers of the Pi Beta Phi women's fraternity opened a school in Gatlinburg. By then the farmers of Gatlinburg had become artisans of considerable variety and talent. What had evolved into a lifestyle for Gatlinburg, became an industry under the tutelage and marketing skills of the "Pi Phis." In addition to providing a ready-made market with their own national chain of gift shops, the Pi Phis opened the Arrowcraft Shop in 1926 as a local outlet for the crafts of Gatlinburg. When the Great Smoky National Park became a reality in 1934, Gatlinburg had been firmly established in the national consciousness as a craftsman's paradise.

As the town began to fill with businesses along Main Street, the naturally reclusive artisans started looking for more room to operate. The first to seek larger, if not greener, pastures was Carl Huskey. He moved about six miles east of town to the Glades, an open area that still had the fertile fields and abundant water the original settlers were looking for when they came in the first place. Carl settled in Whippoorwill Hollow on John's Branch in 1937. He planned and built his home and shop (The Village Craft Shop, which is still there) so that he could pipe water into the buildings. Typical of the artisan's resourcefulness, Carl Huskey had hot running water in his home in 1937; he and his neighbors would wait another 17 years for electricty.

During the next quarter-century, while the national park was turning downtown Gatlinburg into a tourist mecca, the Glades was quietly growing in a different fashion. As the downtown experienced explosive growth in the 1970's, the craft businesses in the Glades were quietly increasing in number. When people from other places learned that an artisan could still make a living in Gatlinburg, the Glades grew to about 15 shops. They brought with them a variety of new pursuits, broadening the town's industrial base. They reached the whopping total of 25 by the end of the 1975 season. In 1978, the artisans of the Glades organized the Great Smoky Arts & Crafts Community with 28 charter members. Of that original group, 12 were still in business under their original ownership at the end of the 1994 season. At the beginning of the 1995 season, 80 shops and studios, along a country road that was once just a pair of wagon ruts, continue to preserve Gatlinburg's craft heritage in the largest settlement of independent artists and craftspeople in North America.

The artisans of the Great Smoky Arts & Crafts Community are maintaining a lifestyle that reminds us of a gentler time. A time when people were measured by the pride which they took in the products of their labor, to a society that expected a high standard of quality.

—Dick McHugh
Historian and Charter Member

APPETIZERS & BEVERAGES

Gatlin County Leather

I originally met Marsha Fountain in her shared studio near the Powdermill complex on Glades Road. There she specialized in hard leather goods such as belts, bags, and wallets. I lost track of her for awhile, but then found she had not only changed locations, but also her specialty. She is now sharing space with Earthspeak, and is producing soft leather goods.

In keeping with Earthspeak's Native American, natural, and mystical theme, she creates beautiful fringed vests and skirts, from natural buckskins, decorated with feathers and hand-beaded. And instead of hard leather purses, these days she makes lovely soft leather medicine bags.

One of Marsha's hobbies is pre-1840's cooking over an open fire. She has a chance to do this when attending rendezvous' for the National Muzzle Loading Rifle Association. She pitches her teepee to sleep in and does all her cooking over an open fire. Before heading off to one of the NMLRA events, she bakes hundreds of cookies and cakes to sell while attending the rendezvous.

Marsha also enjoys cooking at home. She shares with us two of her treasured recipes—**Artichoke Dip** and **The Best Pound Cake**, a family favorite.

Artichoke Dip

Marsha A. Fountain
GATLIN COUNTY LEATHER

Marsha's friend, Judy Poppen, gave her this decadent dip recipe. Marsha likes to serve it with crackers or attack it with a spoon. I like dipping this extremely rich dip with whole wheat pita bread.

2 cans plain artichokes, quartered or chopped

1 cup mayonnaise
1 cup Parmesan cheese, grated

1. Place drained artichokes in bottom of 9" pie plate or shallow casserole.

2. Mix mayonnaise and Parmesan cheese to a paste-like consistency. Spread over the artichokes. Bake at 350° for 15 to 20 minutes until top is starting to brown. Serve hot with crackers.

Avocado Salad (Guacamole)

Gena Lewis
LEWIS FAMILY CRAFTS

Gena serves this on top of lettuce leaves or mixed with lettuce like a salad. Try it with tortilla chips, on toast, as a dressing on a bacon, lettuce, and tomato sandwich, or piped into hollowed cherry tomatoes.

2 ripe avocados, peeled and chopped
1 large ripe tomato, chopped
1 small sweet onion, chopped

1 tablespoon salad oil
2 tablespoons salsa
salt and pepper to taste

1. In a medium bowl, mix the avocados, tomatoes, onion, salad oil, salsa, salt and pepper.

2. Adjust seasonings to your taste, adding more salsa if you like it spicy. Chill for at least 20 minutes before serving.

Future Relics

"Something that has survived the passage of time, especially an object or custom whose original cultural environment has disappeared. Something cherished for its age or association with a person, place, or event; a keepsake." These are the words used in *The American Heritage Dictionary* to describe relic.

Jeff Hale could not have chosen a better name for his gallery. His "Future Relics" ceramic art works may indeed be cherished as a keepsake and passed on to future generations of one's family. His technique of original "Raku" fired and shattered and reconstructed pottery features both historic and contemporary ceramic clocks, vases, and tiles. His award winning work is displayed in galleries across the United States and Canada.

Another resident artist at Future Relics is Jill Adams, a jewelry designer, not to mention innovative cook. She says sometimes Gatlinburg is as remote as an island, because grocery delivery to the area is often delayed. She has learned to stock her pantry so she can come up with her favorite recipes, such as **Refried Bootlegger Beans**, at a moments notice.

Refried Bootlegger Beans

Jill Adams
Future Relics

Jill works with Jeff Hale at Future Relics. Jill's specialty is designing her own line of jewelry. However, she also enjoys creating her own recipes in the kitchen.

She originally created this recipe at home, after a long hike, and discovering their local store was out of bean dip. She now keeps a supply of these ingredients on hand to prepare as a quick appetizer for unexpected company. Jill purchases hot relish from a fellow, who rumor has it is a local moonshine producer. That is why she refers to this as "bootlegger" bean dip.

1 can pinto beans seasoned with pork and onions
1 tablespoon hot relish (salsa)

2 to 3 teaspoons chili powder
¼ teaspoon garlic powder

1. Place pinto beans in food processor, or blender, and puree. Add hot relish, chili powder, and garlic powder. Process until blended with beans.

2. In a small skillet, or saucepan, cook bean mixture on medium heat until you reach desired consistency. Serve warm with corn chips and salsa, or use as a side dish.

Burning Bush Beef & Cheese Balls

Betty Jane Posey
BETTY JANE POSEY GALLERY

These full flavored appetizers are great for a cocktail party, Superbowl get-together, or a church picnic. Make them early in the day or even the night before your party.

8 ounce package cream cheese, softened
1 teaspoon onion juice

½ teaspoon horseradish
2 ½ ounces sliced dried beef (in jar or package)

1. Blend cream cheese with onion juice and horseradish. Shape into small balls.

2. Finely chop dried beef. Roll cheese balls in beef. Refrigerate before serving. Serve on picks or crackers.

Fast and Easy Cheese Puffs

Betty Jane Posey
BETTY JANE POSEY GALLERY

Toss these little cheese puffs into a napkin-lined basket and pass around as an appetizer for a casual gathering, or place them on a silver platter for hors d'oeuvres at a formal cocktail party. This recipe may be made up the day before baking and serving. You may even freeze the unbaked balls for unexpected company or a sudden craving.

½ cup margarine
2 cups grated sharp cheddar cheese (8 ounces)

1 cup sifted flour
1 teaspoon salt

1. Mix and knead all ingredients by hand. Roll into small balls (½" to ¾"). Refrigerate until hard.

2. Preheat oven to 325°. Lightly grease cookie sheet. Place balls 1" apart on sheet and bake for 10 to 12 minutes. Makes 50 to 80 puffs.

Note: To bake frozen balls, place directly from freezer onto lightly greased baking sheet. Bake in preheated 425° oven for 15 minutes.

Deviled Eggs

Gena Lewis
LEWIS FAMILY CRAFTS

"A good mistake of mine," says Gena, "and a favorite of my kids—I never have any leftovers." While testing this recipe, my family of four polished them off in one setting, and agreed with Gena that they were great.

6 eggs, hard-boiled	½ teaspoon mustard
2 teaspoons sweet pickle juice	2 tablespoons relish, chopped onion,
¼ cup salad dressing, or lo-cal	or bacon bits
mayonnaise	bacon bits for garnish

1. Cool and peel eggs. Slice in half and remove yolks.

2. In a small bowl, mash yolks. Add just enough pickle juice to make creamy, but not runny. Add salad dressing and mustard. Fold in your choice of relish, chopped onion or bacon bits.

3. Spoon mixture on top of egg whites and sprinkle additional bacon bits on top. Refrigerate before serving.

"A cheese sandwich tastes like a gourmet meal, if you've hiked a trail on these mountains."

—Charlotte Boles
Whispering Pines

Ham Rolls

Kathy Shields Guttman

For my ninth birthday, my Dad said he would prepare a dinner of my choice. I'm sure he thought I would choose roast beef or fried shrimp (two of my favorites). Without hesitation, I said, "I want ham rolls, meatballs, and raw green peas." He made his famous **Parmesan Meatballs**, shucked peas and sprinkled them with salt, and dispensed with the formality of cutting the ham rolls into pieces. I was in heaven!

Try serving these fun hors d'oeuvres at your next party, or make some up just for your family.

8 ounces cream cheese, softened (see note)

1 tablespoon finely chopped fresh chives, optional

12 slices lean cooked ham, 4" x 6" (packaged or deli)

1 small jar pimentos

12 squares (5" x 5") wax paper

1. Mash cream cheese with a fork to a spreadable consistency. If desired, mix in chives. Pat slices of ham dry with paper towel before spreading with cream cheese.

2. Spread each slice of ham with enough cream cheese to create a thin layer (not too thin—you should not be able to see ham through cream cheese). Place pimento pieces across the top edge (4" edge) of ham. Roll tightly along the 6" edge of ham, starting at the edge with pimento.

3. Place roll on edge of wax paper square. Roll it up and place on plate. Repeat with each roll. Let sit in refrigerator overnight (may be prepared up to 3 days in advance). To serve, remove wax paper. Slice each roll into 3 pieces. Stick toothpick in each piece. Place on serving platter. Makes 36 pieces.

Note: Cream cheese should be purchased in brick form. The soft spreadable cream cheese in a tub does not work well for this recipe—there is too much moisture in it.

Parmesan Meatballs

Kathy Shields Guttman

This is the recipe for my Dad's famous meatballs. He never skimped on garlic. He would chop several cloves at once by smashing them on a chopping board, with the flat side of a knife, and sprinkling liberally with salt before chopping into coarse bits. If you are not that fond of garlic, just cut the amount to your own taste.

1 pound lean ground beef
3 large cloves garlic, peeled and
   chopped
3 green onions, finely chopped
½ teaspoon salt
¼ teaspoon seasoning salt

1 ½ tablespoons Parmesan cheese
¼ cup bread crumbs
1 egg
1 tablespoon olive oil
additional Parmesan cheese

1. In a mixing bowl, combine ground beef, garlic, green onions, salt, seasoning salt, Parmesan cheese, bread crumbs, and egg. Mix together well. Form into small balls.

2. In a large heavy skillet (iron skillet works best), heat olive oil. When oil begins to smoke, add meatballs. Cook, on medium high heat, turning frequently, until brown on all sides, about 12 to 15 minutes. Drain on paper towels and sprinkle generously with more Parmesan cheese. Place a decorated toothpick in each ball and put on platter to serve. Can be served hot or at room temperature. These also go great with spaghetti.

Muller Gallery

Marg C. Muller is known for her original watercolors and limited editions prints. Her work features wildlife, wild flowers, and Smokies landscapes.

Originally from the flat farm land of Oxford, Indiana, Marg comes from a large family of four sisters and eight brothers, all artistically inclined. She says "Since I couldn't wrestle, I decided to go into art." She studied art at Moorehead State University in Kentucky. After working in the advertising business for several years, Marg moved to Gatlinburg and opened her own studio.

Cooking is not included in Marg's list of talents and interests. When building her own home recently, she seriously contemplated leaving out the kitchen. Of course, she did install a kitchen and may occasionally be found in it popping up a batch of her favorite teriyaki flavored popcorn.

Marg's Popcorn

Marg C. Muller
MULLER GALLERY

Marg confesses she does not cook. Her usual fare is take-out. She says "If God wanted me to cook, then why did he create McDonalds?" She does, however, have one specialty that she shares with her cat Rudy—popcorn.

fresh popped popcorn   flaked nutritional yeast
teriyaki sauce, or soy sauce

1. While popcorn is still warm from popping, sprinkle with teriyaki sauce and nutritional yeast. Mix well to coat (teriyaki sauce helps yeast stick to popcorn).

Stuffed Crabmeat Mushrooms

Dean J. Hadden
GREENBRIER RESTAURANT

This versatile recipe can be used as a stuffing for shrimp, steaks, in miniature puff pastries, or simply spread on top of toast and heated. I've adapted the Greenbrier's crabmeat stuffing recipe down to a "household size" portion. It can be doubled, tripled and even quadrupled for a large gathering.

12–15 large mushroom caps   1 teaspoon chives
2 tablespoons melted butter   dash Worcestershire sauce
4 ½ ounces crabmeat, fresh or   1 teaspoon lemon juice
    canned   ¼ teaspoon lemon pepper
1 egg   ¼ teaspoon granulated garlic
2 teaspoons sour cream   1 cup crushed croutons

1. Remove stems and clean mushrooms. Melt butter in 7" x 11" baking dish and gently roll mushrooms in melted butter and place in dish.

2. Chop crabmeat. Mix with egg, sour cream, chives, Worcestershire sauce, lemon juice, lemon pepper, and garlic. Add crushed croutons. Mix well.

3. Top each mushroom with stuffing. Bake at 350° for 15 to 20 minutes. Serve hot.

Shrimp & Cheese Gem

Mac McDonell
GEMSTONE

This makes an impressive centerpiece to grace a buffet table; or, place on your coffee table while you gather to watch "the big game" on television.

Use a variety of your favorite cheeses: cheddar, colby, brick, Muenster, havarti, and marble.

Cabbage with Shrimp, Cheese & Olives

1 large head of cabbage
1 can medium size pitted ripe olives
1 jar green olives
1 package sharp cheese, cut in ½" cubes

1 package mellow white cheese, cut in ½" cubes
36 to 40 medium shrimp, boiled, peeled, and cooled
1 box toothpicks

Cocktail Sauce

1 ½ to 2 cups ketchup
1 teaspoon horseradish (or more to taste)

juice from 1 lemon wedge
dash of Worcestershire sauce

1. Slice a thin layer off bottom of cabbage to set it level on serving plate. Slice off top ¼ of cabbage and hollow out center to hold cocktail sauce.

2. Beginning at top edge of cabbage, begin alternating olives, cheese, and shrimp on toothpicks. To achieve maximum volume, pin first layer tight against the cabbage. Then layer by sticking toothpicks out a bit further from cabbage each time. Work your way around cabbage in circles until cabbage is full.

3. Fill cabbage with cocktail sauce. Place on serving plate. Cover with plastic wrap and refrigerate.

4. To prepare cocktail sauce: Mix together ketchup, horseradish, lemon juice, and Worcesteshire sauce.

Orange Julius

Martha Powers
OSTEEN & POWERS

When Martha's young niece and nephews came to visit, they always asked for this frothy thirst quencher. Now that they are grown, they still do!

⅓ cup frozen orange juice concentrate
½ cup milk
½ cup water

¼ cup sugar
½ teaspoon vanilla
5 or 6 ice cubes

1. Combine orange juice, milk, water, sugar, vanilla, and ice in a blender. Cover and blend just until smooth (about 30 seconds). Serve immediately. Makes 3 cups.

Variation: Try making this with different frozen juice concentrates, such as orange-pineapple or raspberry.

Sharing. When dividing a piece of candy (or any other treat for children), let one child divide the slice and the other gets first choice.

—Clarice Maples
Hemlock Falls Nightly Rentals

Osteen & Powers

Originally from different parts of Georgia, Martha Powers and Becky Osteen are charter members of the Great Smoky Arts & Crafts Community. Baskets are Martha's specialty. Their studio is well stocked with traditional and contemporary baskets by the area's finest basket makers.

Some baskets may be described as functional, and some as works of art. They have picnic baskets, staircase baskets, Nantucket baskets, egg baskets, miniature baskets, and random weave baskets of aluminum and acrylic; not to mention woven leather baskets and contemporary baskets made of telephone wire and copper metal. After seeing all their beautiful baskets, if you are so inclined, you may purchase one of their basket kits and make your own.

Becky's specialty these days is golf. A separate small room of the studio is what they refer to as the "19th Hole." For sale are golf gifts such as golf ball candles, serving trays with handpainted tiles, Cosby Caddies (cute teddy bear caddies), duffer bibs and towels, and of course, golf related handpainted baskets.

Martha also weaves magic in the kitchen with her delicious recipes; and, when you feel like a "basketcase," Becky has a "secret potion" to cure what ails you the morning after.

Whiskey "On the Rocks"

Becky Osteen
OSTEEN & POWERS

Becky is not exactly fond of spending time cooking in the kitchen. However, she has some creative ideas on how to mix whiskey and bread crumbs. This is Becky's idea of a great recipe for an enjoyable Smoky Mountain afternoon.

1 bottle whiskey   **bread crumbs**

1. Take a drive out to Greenbrier Road. Find a parking spot along the river. Wade out to biggest rock in the creek. Drink whiskey on the rocks and throw bread crumbs to the fish.

Note: If you try this "tongue-in-cheek" recipe, see Becky's following recipe for **Tomato Juice & Crackers**; you may need it. This is one of the few recipes I did not test for this cookbook—you are on your own. The writer and publisher takes no responsibility if you try this one.

Tomato Juice & Crackers

Becky Osteen
OSTEEN & POWERS

You might call this a companion recipe to Whiskey "On the Rocks." Becky says, "Eat and enjoy—no need to chew—great for a quick breakfast, especially the morning after."

Becky prefers using Hunts Tomato Juice and Waverly Wafer Crackers for this concoction. She says "If you substitute, it will not taste as good."

1 ¼ cups cold tomato juice   **4 ounces crackers**

1. Crush crackers into large bowl. Pour very cold tomato juice over crackers and mix well. Mixture should be soggy. Eat with a spoon.

Russian Coffee

Betty Jane Posey
BETTY JANE POSEY GALLERY

Brew up a batch of this mocha treat the next time Mother Nature gives us the cold shoulder.

½ cup sugar
¼ cup water
½ ounce semi-sweet chocolate
⅛ teaspoon salt

½ cup whole milk
½ cup whipping cream
2 cups very strong hot coffee
1 teaspoon vanilla

1. Heat sugar, water, chocolate, and salt in a saucepan over low heat, stirring frequently, until chocolate melts.

2. Stir in milk and whipping cream. Heat until hot. Add coffee, beat until foamy, and then stir in vanilla. Serve in pre-warmed coffee cups. Makes four 6 ounce servings.

Tea Time Toddy

Betty Jane Posey
BETTY JANE POSEY GALLERY

Betty Jane says, "This toddy is good for colds, flu, tiredness, or just a great afternoon pick-me-up."

4 cups strongly brewed tea
8 whole cloves
4 lemon slices, plus 4 more for
    garnish

4 tablespoons honey
1 teaspoon grated orange rind
½ teaspoon allspice
6 ounces bourbon

1. In a saucepan, heat tea along with cloves, 4 lemon slices, honey, orange rind, and allspice. Mix well and gently simmer (do not boil) for 5 minutes.

2. Pour 1 ½ ounces of bourbon into 4 pre-warmed mugs. Fill mugs to the top with tea, poured through a strainer. Top each serving with a lemon slice.

Soups & Salads

Chablis Cheddar Soup

Cindy Black
THE WILD PLUM TEA ROOM

On a cold winter's day in March, I had the pleasure of consuming this rich creamy soup at the Wild Plum Tea Room. When testing this recipe at home, I was amazed at how easy and quick it was to prepare this satisfying soup.

¼ cup butter
1 bunch green onions, chopped
2 chicken bouillon cubes
2 cans cheddar soup

½ cup Chablis wine
1 cup water
1 cup half and half cream
slivered almonds

1. Melt butter in a saucepan. Saute green onions and bouillon cubes until tender and cubes are dissolved.

2. Add cheddar soup, wine, water, and cream. Stir until smooth. Cook on medium until thoroughly heated. Serve with slivered almonds on top. Serves 4 to 6.

"I enjoy meeting people and becoming the 'personal potter' to many of them. Some of the biggest joys in my work is to see the look on peoples' faces when they get a bowl 'just the right size,' or a mug that fits 'just perfect ... no one else better use it, or else' (this aside to a spouse)."

—Buie Boling
Buie Pottery

Chicken Soup

Kathy Shields Guttman

What is a cookbook without a recipe for Chicken Soup? I could not resist sharing my recipe for this time-honored soup. When I first got married, I could barely boil water, let alone make soup. My mother-in-law, Jean Guttman, showed me how to make her son's favorite soup. I've adapted her recipe, slightly, by leaving out parsley and skinning the chicken. My husband says he likes my soup better. Is that because he lives with me now, instead of his mother?

1 whole chicken, cut into pieces	1 whole onion, peeled
2 ½ quarts water	4 sprigs fresh dill
3 carrots, sliced into 2" chunks	2 tablespoons salt
2 celery stalks, sliced into 2" chunks	pepper
celery leaves	

1. Remove skin and fat from chicken pieces. Place in a large soup pot. Pour boiling water on top of chicken and place on medium-high heat. Bring water back to a boil and skim off the dirty froth that rises to the top of the broth.

2. Add carrots, celery, celery leaves, onion, dill, salt, and pepper. Reduce heat and simmer for 1 ½ hours. Remove from heat and allow soup to sit with vegetables and chicken for 1 hour. Remove celery, celery leaves, onion, and dill from soup and discard. Remove chicken from soup (may be served separately or debone and freeze for use in another recipe).

3. Serve chicken broth in bowl with chunks of carrot. I like to serve this soup with egg noodles or matzo balls. Serves 8 to 10.

Cream of Peanut Soup

Betty Jane Posey

BETTY JANE POSEY GALLERY

If you love peanut butter, you will go nuts over this delightfully different soup. It has a taste that reminds me of eating peanut butter stuffed celery.

2 tablespoons butter
¼ cup minced onion
⅔ cup chopped celery and leaves
3 tablespoons flour
4 cups chicken broth

½ cup peanut butter
1 cup half and half cream
salt and pepper to taste
salted peanuts

1. Melt butter in saucepan. Add onion and celery. Cook until tender, but not brown. Remove from heat and blend in flour.

2. Gradually add chicken broth and bring to a boil over medium heat, stirring constantly. Blend in peanut butter. Stir in cream and seasonings. Heat slowly, do not boil. Garnish with salted peanuts. Serves 4 to 6.

"It was like blind faith. I'd sit down, without any idea of what I was doing, and trust that a landscape was going to come out. It would come out, and somebody would come along and buy it. Every time that would happen, it was like another miracle. I thought, 'Well, this will go away, it won't be as miraculous.' Over 25 years later it's still miraculous!"

—Betty Jane Posey
Betty Jane Posey Gallery

Onion Soup

Betty Jane Posey

BETTY JANE POSEY GALLERY

When raw, onions are often described as having a sharp, stinging, stinky aroma. Cook them and, suddenly, their scent is transformed into a sweet, savory fragrance.

The delectable scent of this soup will have everyone asking "When's dinner?"

2 ½ cups thinly sliced onions	2 beef bouillon cubes
2 tablespoons melted bacon drippings	¼ teaspoon pepper
2 cans condensed beef bouillon	12 rounds sliced French bread
2 cans water	¼ cup grated Parmesan cheese

1. Saute onions in bacon drippings until tender, about 5 minutes. Slowly add beef bouillon and water. Heat until simmering. Add bouillon cubes and pepper. Stir well and cover. Cook for 20 minutes.

2. Sprinkle sliced bread rounds with Parmesan cheese and place under broiler until brown. Top each serving of soup with 2 bread rounds. Serves 6.

Mushroom Bisque

Dave Howard
SPICED PEAR CAFE

Formerly a chef at the Buckhorn Inn, Dave and his wife Annie have opened up their own restaurant. Dave has his own philosophy when it comes to cooking and recipes. He rarely follows a recipe exactly as written. He tells people to use recipes as a guide, using the best ingredients you like and have on hand.

For this recipe, and for Dave's **Tomato-Basil Bisque**, I've departed from my usual style of writing recipes and have written them in Dave's own format.

2 bay leaves	2 tablespoons chopped garlic
1 pound sliced mushrooms	2 tablespoons chopped shallots
1 medium onion, sliced or diced	2 stalks sliced celery

Saute above ingredients in a little olive oil or butter until onions are limp and transparent. Add:

1 cup red wine, or Marsala wine, or sherry	1 cup chicken stock or broth, or beef, or veal stock
	2 cups water and bring to a hard boil.

Boil until ½ the volume of liquid is reduced.

Add 1 quart heavy cream and bring to a boil. After cream boils, reduce heat and let simmer until cream naturally thickens and sweetens soup. Season to taste with salt, pepper, and thyme. Serves 8 to 10.

Note: To lighten the recipe you may substitue skim milk, 2% milk, whole milk, or light cream for the heavy cream. Do not use half & half. Dave says it tends to break down in soups.

Tomato-Basil Bisque

Dave Howard
SPICED PEAR CAFE

Another of Dave's mouth-watering soups. It really is excellent. I know some of you may be scared off by the heavy cream, but do not let it stop you. Consider it a special occasion recipe and forget about the calories and cholesterol—you can eat low-fat meals next week.

1 medium onion, sliced or diced	2 tablespoons chopped shallots
2 tablespoons chopped garlic	2 bay leaves

Saute above ingredients in a little olive oil or butter until onions are limp and transparent. Add:

1 full handful of chopped fresh basil	2 cups red wine

Bring to a hard boil until ½ the wine's volume is reduced. Add:

1 cup chicken stock or broth	2 cups pureed tomatoes
2 cups diced tomatoes	1 cup water

Bring to a hard boil again and let boil until all flavors are mixed well. Add:

1 quart heavy cream

and bring to boil. Let simmer until cream naturally thickens soup. Season to taste with sugar, salt, pepper, and sage. Serves 8 to 10.

Pumpkin Soup

Pat Thomas
FIBER CREATIONS INC.

Pat enjoys making homemade soups. They go great on cold Smoky Mountain nights. This recipe conjures up, in my mind, a picture of crisp fall days with leaves turning crimson, orange, and yellow; and pumpkin patches ready to harvest for pies, soups, and jack-o-lanterns.

2 tablespoons butter
1 small onion, chopped
½ teaspoon ginger
¼ teaspoon thyme
1 tablespoon flour

2 cups pumpkin (canned, or fresh cooked)
2 cups chicken broth
2 cups milk
salt and pepper

1. Melt butter in 2 quart saucepan. Saute onion on medium-low heat for 5 minutes. Add ginger and thyme. Stir in flour. Add pumpkin and continue cooking for 5 minutes.

2. Slowly stir in chicken broth and milk. Bring to a gentle boil, then cover and reduce heat to a simmer for 5 minutes. Season with salt and pepper. Serves 4.

Shrimp and Mushroom Chowder

Pat Thomas
FIBER CREATIONS INC.

A steaming hot bowl of this rich chowder will warm you up on a cold winter night. On a hot summer day, let a chilled version of this chowder cool you down.

2 cups chopped raw shrimp
1 pound fresh mushrooms, sliced
1 ½ cups water
½ teaspoon salt, plus 1 teaspoon
¼ cup butter
1 small onion, chopped

¼ cup flour
¼ teaspoon freshly ground pepper
2 ½ cups whole milk
½ cup whipping cream
parsley for garnish

1. Cook shrimp in boiling water, until they turn pink, about 1 ½ to 2 minutes. Drain and set aside.

2. In a saucepan, combine mushrooms, water, and ½ teaspoon salt. Bring to a boil. Cover and reduce heat to a simmer for 10 minutes. Drain mushrooms, reserving liquid, and set aside.

3. Melt butter in saucepan. Saute onions until tender. While stirring, add flour, 1 teaspoon salt, and pepper. Mix well. Slowly stir in reserved liquid, blending until smooth. Add milk gradually. Cook over medium heat, stirring constantly, until mixture comes to a boil and thickens.

4. Remove from heat. Stir in cream, shrimp, and mushrooms. If serving cold, chill thoroughly before serving. Garnish with parsley. If serving hot, return to a low heat for a few minutes until cream, shrimp, and mushrooms are heated through. Do not let boil.

Summer Vegetable Soup

Buckhorn Inn

Winter, spring, summer or fall, I know you will enjoy this unusual soup all year round. Even if you are not a fan of eggplant, try it in this soup. I think you will be converted.

2 quarts beef stock	1 medium zucchini, shredded
2 pounds mushrooms, sliced	2 tablespoons flour
1 medium eggplant, peeled and diced	2 tablespoons lemon juice
2 medium yellow squash, diced	1 tablespoon oregano
1 onion, diced	1 teaspoon white pepper

1. In a large soup pot, combine the beef stock, mushrooms, eggplant, yellow squash, and onion. Bring to a boil and boil for 5 minutes.

2. In a large bowl, combine the zucchini, flour, lemon juice, oregano, and white pepper. Add this mixture to the boiling soup and reduce the heat to a simmer for 1 hour. Serves 6 to 8.

March Blizzard

"The great blizzard of 1993 caused 18 guests staying at The Buckhorn Inn to have an extended stay. Four days later, when all of the guests had departed except two, the Wilsons, we relaxed for a memorable evening. The Wilsons cooked dinner for all of us who had worked hard making everyone else comfortable.

The long table glowed with candle light. The fire crackled in the background. The world outside was silent. The conversation inside was subdued, yet joyful. We were family, neighbors, and friends. We toasted to the experience, and … to Spring!"

—John Burns
Buckhorn Inn

Zucchini Soup

Buckhorn Inn

This rich creamy soup is deceiving in its taste and appearance. One might think it has an abundance of fat and calories and took all day to prepare. The fact is, it is low in calories and may be quickly and easily prepared in less than an hour.

1 cup water
8 small zucchini, sliced
1 small onion, minced
2 tablespoons chicken bouillon
    granules
2 teaspoons Season-All Salt

1 teaspoon fresh parsley
¼ cup cornstarch
3 cups milk
2 tablespoons butter
2 tablespoons chicken bouillon
    granules

1. Place the water, zucchini, onion, bouillon granules, Season-All Salt, and parsley in a medium saucepan. Cook on medium heat until tender, approximately 15 minutes.

2. Put the cornstarch in a small bowl. Slowly stir in small amount of the milk, mixing until all of the cornstarch is dissolved.

3. In a separate saucepan combine the cornstarch mixture, remaining milk, butter, and additional bouillon granules. Simmer over medium heat, stirring occasionally, until the mixture is thickened.

4. Puree the zucchini mixture in a blender or food processor and add it to thickened broth. Serves 8.

Wild Plum Tea Room

*I*magine yourself on a hot sultry day, sitting at a table for two on a charming little screened porch surrounded by shade. You have a glass of the best iced tea you have ever tasted, you are spreading Wild Plum Jelly on miniature Wild Plum Muffins and looking out at the country road. A breeze floats by and you feel totally relaxed and refreshed.

Or, on a cold winter's day, you sit inside this cozy little tea room with its batten board walls and lace window curtains and enjoy the aroma and taste of a piping hot cup of their same Wild Plum tea, while gazing at the paintings on the wall depicting Smoky Mountain scenery.

No matter what season, The Wild Plum Tea Room serves outstanding homemade soups, salads, and sandwiches developed by their manager, Cindy Freeman Black. Her specialty is creating desserts (one of my favorites in the summer is the Peach Schnapps Sundae). They are some of the most delectable desserts in Tennessee. Cindy has written her own cookbook entitled *All My Best Recipes* and it is available for sale in the tea room's gift shop.

Cindy enjoys using fresh ingredients and fresh herbs from their herb garden for the tea room. When deciding which recipes to contribute to this cookbook, she thought I might like two of her "fun and fast" recipes, **Chablis Cheddar Soup** and **Tomato French Onion Soup**.

Tomato French Onion Soup

Cindy Black
THE WILD PLUM TEA ROOM

One of the most popular soups served at The Wild Plum, Cindy is often asked for the recipe. "It is so easy," she says, "I am usually too embarrassed to give out the recipe."

Easy to make, the **Homemade Croutons** add a classy touch to this soup. Throw together a salad, toss in these croutons and you've got a simple and satisfying meal.

Soup

½ cup butter
2 large yellow or Vidalia onions, sliced
2 cans tomato soup

2 cans French onion soup
1 cup red wine
homemade croutons
Parmesan cheese

Homemade Croutons

1 loaf French bread, cubed
½ cup butter, melted

4 tablespoons Pinch of Herbs seasoning mix

1. In a 2 quart saucepan, melt butter. Saute onions until tender, about 5 minutes. Add tomato soup, French onion soup, and red wine. Heat thoroughly.

2. Spoon into soup bowls. Top with croutons and sprinkle with Parmesan cheese. Serves 6.

3. To prepare croutons: Preheat oven to 350°. Place bread cubes on baking sheet. Melt butter and mix in Pinch of Herbs (or your own favorite mix of dried herbs). Pour over bread cubes. Bake for 20 to 25 minutes.

Fresh Broccoli Salad

Connie Alewine
ALEWINE POTTERY

If you present this colorful crunchy salad in one of Robert Alewine's beautiful pottery bowls, you will have a treat to delight your sense of sight and taste.

1 bunch fresh broccoli	simulated bacon)
½ cup shredded carrots	½ cup mayonnaise
½ cup shredded cheddar cheese	2 to 3 tablespoons sugar
2 strips cooked bacon, crumbled (or	1 ½ tablespoons red wine vinegar

1. Cut broccoli into flowerettes. Plunge into boiling water for 10 seconds. Drain and dip into ice water to stop cooking process. Drain well. Add carrots, cheddar cheese, and bacon to broccoli.

2. Prepare dressing by whisking together mayonnaise, sugar, and red wine vinegar. Pour dressing over salad and chill well before serving.

"My favorite hike in the Smokies is from my shop to the bank. Sometimes the path gets overgrown, but I remember the way."

—Robert Alewine
Alewine Pottery

Cornbread Salad

Gena Lewis
LEWIS FAMILY CRAFTS

This recipe, and the following garbanzo and kidney bean salads, are from one of Gena and Mike's favorite restaurants, The Log Cabin, situated between Newport and Cosby, Tennessee. It is a family owned restaurant. The family have been in the area for about 150 years. Gena says, "These are country people cooking fresh country foods and it is one of the friendliest places in the Smokies."

1 ½ to 2 cups cornbread, crumbled
2 tablespoons bacon bits
2 tablespoons onion, chopped

2 tablespoons celery, chopped
1 tablespoon relish, drained
mayonnaise

1. Mix together ingredients with enough mayonnaise to make it stick, but not enough to soak cornbread.

Garbanzo Bean Salad (Chick Pea)

2 cups cooked garbanzo beans
   (may use canned)
2 tablespoons celery, chopped

2 tablespoons green onion, chopped
1 tablespoon sweet relish
2 tablespoons mayonnaise

1. Mix together and refrigerate a few hours.

Kidney Bean Salad

2 cups kidney beans
2 tablespoons celery, chopped
2 tablespoons onion, chopped

1 tablespoon sweet relish
2 tablespoons mayonnaise.

1. Mix together and refrigerate for a few hours.

Herbed Peas

Gena Lewis
LEWIS FAMILY CRAFTS

An easy low calorie dish for summer meals. It keeps well in the frig for a few days, and is perfect for make-ahead meals or picnics. This recipe was given to Gena by Lee Nelson, a lady from El Paso, Texas.

2 packs frozen peas, 10 ounces each
⅔ cup pickled onions, finely sliced
⅓ cup lo-cal French dressing

½ teaspoon dill weed
lettuce leaves, cleaned and dryed

1. Cook and chill peas. Add pickled onions, French dressing and dill weed. Toss lightly.

2. Allow to sit 24 hours in refrigerator so peas can season. Serve on individual lettuce leaves.

Pasta House Salad

Gena Lewis
LEWIS FAMILY CRAFTS

Gena adapted this recipe from the Pasta House restaurant in St. Louis, Missouri. She sometimes substitutes a lo-cal Italian dressing for the oil and vinegar. Try this lovely salad at your next picnic, brunch or "company's coming" dinner.

1 head Romaine lettuce
1 head iceberg lettuce
¼ cup pimentos
½ cup marinated artichoke hearts

½ purple onion, sliced
½ cup oil
¼ cup red wine vinegar
¼ cup Parmesan cheese

1. Clean and break up lettuce into pieces. Drain and dry. Place prepared lettuce in a salad bowl. Top with pimentos, marinated artichokes, and purple onion.

2. In a separate bowl, whisk together oil and vinegar. Add Parmesan cheese. Whisk until well mixed. Pour over salad. Toss and serve.

Pomegranate Orange Salad

Kathy Shields Guttman

Prepare this salad in the late fall when the leaves have fallen and the sky is grey. The sparkling ruby red pomegranate and the shimmering orange mandarin sections add some much needed color for an otherwise bleak November day.

Salad

- 1 small head red leaf lettuce
- 1 small head Boston lettuce
- 1 cup thinly sliced red onion
- 1 pomegranate
- 1 small can mandarin orange sections, drained

Vinaigrette Dressing

- 2 tablespoons tarragon white wine vinegar
- 1 tablespoon olive oil
- 1 teaspoon honey
- ¼ cup orange juice
- 1 teaspoon Dijon mustard
- 1 clove garlic, minced
- 1 green onion, minced
- 2 tablespoons chopped fresh parsley

1. In a large salad bowl, combine red lettuce, Boston lettuce, and red onion.

2. Break pomegranate into sections and remove red fruit. Add to salad along with orange sections. Just before serving toss with vinaigrette.

3. To prepare vinaigrette: Whisk together vinegar, oil, honey, orange juice, and mustard. Add garlic, green onion, and parsley and mix well. Chill before using.

"On Mt. Le Conte the whole world seems spread beneath your feet."
—Annetta Hendrickson
Leather Works

Buckhorn Handcrafts

*J*ake and Lorraine Quilliams met in Newfoundland while Jake was serving in the military. I wonder if Lorraine ever imagined as she was growing up in that Canadian island province that one day she would make her life in the American South? Or that she would marry a native of Gatlinburg and enter a fine tradition of making crafts?

The Quilliams have been operating their craft shop on Buckhorn Road seven days a week now for many years. Framed on the wall and dated April 1, 1978, is the first dollar they made selling their handcrafted goods. Child size wooden tool boxes with miniature wooden tools, doll cribs and dolls, and other toys are just some of their crafts that will please the young. For the slightly older customer there are quilts, linens, baskets, and more.

Lorraine leads a typical Smoky Mountain life. In addition to the craft business, she keeps active at their church. A favorite recipe of hers to take to the church picnics is **Seven Layer Salad**. But my favorite recipe contributed by Lorraine is her **Zucchini Rounds**. These little morsels are absolutely delicious.

Seven Layer Salad

Lorraine Quilliams
BUCKHORN HANDCRAFTS

This is a wonderful make-ahead salad. By sealing the layers with mayonnaise overnight, all the flavors get a chance to mix, mingle, and meld together. It also keeps the lettuce fresh and crisp. Lorraine says this is a big hit at their church picnics.

1 large iceberg lettuce, rinsed and dryed

8 ounce can peas, drained, or frozen peas, defrosted

1 purple onion, sliced thin

4 hardboiled eggs, sliced

1 pound bacon, cooked, drained well, and chopped

1 cup mayonnaise

Parmesan cheese, grated

1. In a large salad bowl, layer the lettuce, then the peas, the purple onion, the hardboiled eggs, and then the bacon.

2. Spread mayonnaise on top of bacon layer, making sure to seal the salad to the edges. Sprinkle grated Parmesan cheese on top. Cover with plastic wrap and place in refrigerator overnight. Just before serving, toss lightly, or serve as a wedge in its layered form.

Turtle Hollow Caesar Salad

Ross Markley

THE WOODTURNER & BASKET SHOP

Of course a crafter who turns Appalachian hardwoods into rich beautiful salad bowls, would contribute an equally rich incredible recipe for Caesar Salad. The Gorgonzola (a type of Blue Cheese) gives this classic Caesar a special touch. Ross makes this "to slim down after eating **Woodturner's' Chili.**" I hate to break this to you Ross, but this salad is not low-cal. However, it is the best Caesar I have ever tasted. Serve it with your Chili and diet next week.

1 clove garlic, peeled	chilled Romaine (1 or 2 bunches
2 cloves garlic, minced	depending on size)
⅓ cup olive oil	2 eggs, coddled (see note)
1 ½ teaspoons Worcestershire sauce	½ cup Parmesan cheese
½ teaspoon dry mustard	1 ½ cups Gorgonzola cheese, cut in
½ teaspoon salt	small chunks
½ teaspoon coarse ground pepper	garlic croutons

1. Rub wooden salad bowl with peeled garlic. Add minced garlic, olive oil, Worcestershire sauce, dry mustard, salt, and pepper. Mix thoroughly with wooden spurtle (see note).

2. Tear Romaine into pieces and add to bowl. Toss with wooden salad servers. Break eggs into salad. Add Parmesan and Gorgonzola. Toss again. Add croutons and toss lightly.

Notes: 1. To coddle eggs, drop raw eggs, still in their shell, into boiling water for 1 minute. Remove.

2. The wooden spurtle (a round wooden stirring stick) works beautifully for mixing the dressing, without scratching your wooden salad bowl. However, if you do not own a spurtle, a wooden spoon works almost as well.

Vat of Macaroni Salad

Mac McDonell
GEMSTONE

This hefty salad makes enough to feed two dozen or more people. When the McDonells and McHughs have their annual 4th of July celebration, Mac serves this along with grilled hot dogs and sausage, various chips and dips, fruit salad, and homemade cookies. Make this up for your next barbecue or picnic. For extra flavor, try making this with the recipe for **Homemade Mayonnaise** found in this book.

1 large box macaroni, cooked, drained, and cooled
12 large hard boiled eggs (10 chopped, 2 sliced)
1 medium onion, finely chopped
1 medium green pepper, diced
1 ½ cup chopped celery
½ cup sweet relish, optional
mayonnaise
salt and pepper
paprika and parsley for garnish

1. Place cooked macaroni in a large mixing bowl. Add chopped eggs, onion, green pepper, celery, and sweet relish (if desired). Add mayonnaise, salt, and pepper to taste and desired consistency. Mix well.

2. Decorate the top with round slices of egg and sprigs of parsley. Lightly sprinkle with paprika. Refrigerate.

"Every July 4th, for the past 14 years, we meet at the pond where we live, for a barbecue and fireworks display put on by Mac McDonell and Dick McHugh. Lots of friends, family, and neighbors gather for this annual event. We shoot the fireworks off over the pond and 'ooh and aah,' while our neighbor, whose house is on the other side of the pond, sits on his deck with a tennis racket waiting for any misguided fireworks."

—Susan McDonell
Gemstone

Homemade Mayonnaise

Betty Jane Posey
BETTY JANE POSEY GALLERY

Once you have tried making your own mayonnaise and discover how easy it is, and its superior taste, you'll never again be satisfied with commercial mayonnaise. Try Betty Jane's recipe first, then experiment with different vinegars and herbs to create new versions.

2 egg yolks
juice of 1 lemon
1 tablespoon vinegar
1 teaspoon prepared mustard

1 teaspoon salt
red pepper to taste
2 cups vegetable oil

1. Combine egg yolks, lemon juice, vinegar, mustard, salt, and red pepper. Slowly pour in oil to mixture and beat until firm. This is fast when prepared in a food processor. It may also be done with an electric beater or whisk.

Honey Mustard Salad Dressing

Sara Kane
ADOUGHABLE THINGS BY NANCY

This tangy sweet dressing is great on your favorite mix of salad greens. While testing, I found it also worked well as a spread with sandwich fixings and as a coating on chicken pieces (see my recipe for **Honey Mustard Chicken Breasts**). Add papaya, kiwi fruit, and sliced red onion to salad greens, mix in a bit of fresh or bottled lime juice to this dressing, and you have an exotic and delicious salad.

½ cup mayonnaise
2 tablespoons Dijon mustard
2 tablespoons honey

2 ¾ tablespoons oil
garlic powder and cayenne to taste

1. Whisk together all the above ingredients. Store in air-tight container in refrigerator.

Tahini Dressing

Mary Louise Hunt
FIBER CREATIONS

I had a hard time deciding into which category to fit this versatile recipe. Should I put it under Appetizers? It makes an incredible dip for raw vegetables and/or pita bread. Should I put it under Sauces? Mary Louise says this may be used as a sauce or spread. You may fill a pita pocket with cucumber slices and top with this sauce; even put it on falafel, or use as a dipping sauce for chicken nuggets.

I finally decided to put it under Salad Dressings. It has a thin consistency, and it is called a dressing. Add a little extra lemon juice and it makes a great salad dressing. If you want a thicker consistency to use as a spread or dip, use ¼ cup less water in the recipe.

½ cup tahini	2 tablespoons tamari (soy sauce)
¼ cup oil	½ cup water
juice of one lemon	freshly grated gingeroot, optional

1. In a small mixing bowl, blend tahini with oil, lemon juice, and tamari. Whisk together well.

2. Add water a few spoonfuls at a time, whisking until smooth (add water until you reach desired consistency). Let stand for 20 minutes, or more, before serving. Gingeroot may be added for extra pizzazz.

"Greggorys Bald is neat with the Azaleas blooming and blueberries for the picking, but watch out for the bears."

—Otto Preske
Otto Preske—Artist in Wood

Herbed Vinegars

Frances Fox
FIBER CREATIONS

These vinegars are truly a work of art. The beautiful color hues created by combining different herbs and vinegar, look fantastic placed in a pretty bottle. Their beauty is only surpassed by their great taste. Try Frances' suggested combinations below, or experiment with your own ideas. These make wonderful gifts for your friends and family.

- white wine vinegar or 5% vinegar
- fresh cinnamon basil and cinnamon sticks
- fresh mint, lemon balm, and lemon slices
- fresh green & red hot pepper and

- garlic cloves
- fresh oregano and garlic cloves
- fresh rosemary and thyme
- fresh garlic blossoms
- fresh chive blossoms (beautiful lavender color)

1. Heat vinegar (do not boil) and pour over fresh herbs in a big round sterilized jar. Let sit at room temperature for 3 weeks.

2. Strain vinegar and re-bottle in sterilized pretty bottles with fresh herbs (same variety as originally used). Seal with cork or screw top. Discard strained herbs.

Plant basil with tomatoes. To keep slugs away from basil, surround them with eggshells. Plant mint under apple trees.

—Frances Fox
Fiber Creations

Quick Breads, Muffins, & Pancakes

Banana Bread

Garnet Weiss
Woods by Weiss

Garnet's recipe for banana bread was handed down to her from her mother, Jane Holdcraft. Most families have their own version of this black speckled treat. If you do not have your own family recipe, or are ready to try a new one, give Garnet's a try!

1 cup sugar	3 tablespoons sour milk
½ cup shortening	2 cups flour
3 mashed bananas (about 1 cup)	½ teaspoon baking powder
2 eggs, beaten	¼ teaspoon salt
1 teaspoon baking soda	

1. Cream together sugar and shortening. Mix in bananas and eggs. Dissolve baking soda in sour milk. Sift together flour, baking powder, and salt. Mix in dry ingredients alternately with milk.

2. Pour batter into a greased 9" x 5" loaf pan and allow to stand 20 minutes before baking. Preheat oven to 350°. Bake loaf for 50 minutes or until done.

To get ballpoint ink off clothes, spray spot with hairspray and wash as usual.

—Garnet Weiss
Woods By Weiss

Pumpkin Bread

Wilma Prebor
QUILTS BY WILMA

Wilma baked this recipe in three 1 pound coffee cans that had been greased and floured. When testing this recipe, I used two 9" x 5" loaf pans. Either way you slice it, round or rectangle, I think you'll agree that this is a moist and tasty loaf.

3 cups sugar
1 cup vegetable oil
3 eggs
1 ¾ cups canned pumpkin
3 cups flour
1 teaspoon salt

½ teaspoon baking soda
1 teaspoon baking powder
1 teaspoon each of cinnamon, cloves, and nutmeg
½ cup chopped nuts

1. Preheat oven to 350°. Grease and flour two 9" x 5" loaf pans or 3 coffee cans.

2. In a large mixing bowl beat together sugar, vegetable oil, and eggs. Beat in pumpkin.

3. Sift together flour, salt, baking soda, baking powder, cinnamon, cloves, and nutmeg. Combine with above ingredients. Stir in nuts. Pour into prepared pans and bake for 90 minutes. Freezes well.

Fiber Creations Inc.

*T*his gallery was originally established as a cooperative of five weavers in 1988. It now has eight artisans working in a variety of media expressions. In addition to weavers and fiber artists, others specialize in photography, marbled watercolor paper and calligraphy, fused and slumped glass, stained glass, jewelry, quilting, smocking, applique, toys, and tatting.

Three members of the co-op have contributed recipes to this book. Their recipes are as different as their chosen craft.

A Gatlinburg native, Frances Fox, is a fiber artist who has work displayed in art galleries across the South. Her talent in fiber is "woven" into her genes. Both of her grandmothers were weavers. Her recipe for **Harvest Loaf Cake** is a delectable concoction of pumpkin, spices, and chocolate chips with a cinnamon glaze.

Mary-Louise Hunt is a glass painter and designer. Her paintings and glass have been included in exhibitions across North America and Italy. Her **Alu Sabje**, curried potatoes, reflect her time spent in India.

Pat Thomas is a fiber artist, in addition to her calligraphy and marbled watercolor paper. Her **Shrimp and Mushroom Chowder** is soothing for both summer and winter, as it may be served hot or cold.

Harvest Loaf Cake

Frances Fox
FIBER CREATIONS INC.

The combination of pumpkin, chocolate, nuts, and spice makes this an incredibly moist, dense, and delicious loaf. Frances serves this loaf during the annual Great Smoky Arts & Crafts Community's Heritage Days open house in October.

Loaf

½ cup margarine, softened
1 cup sugar
2 eggs
1 ¾ cups flour
1 teaspoon baking soda
½ teaspoon salt
1 teaspoon cinnamon

½ teaspoon nutmeg
¼ teaspoon ginger
¼ teaspoon ground cloves
16 ounce can pumpkin
¾ cup chopped nuts, divided
¾ cup chocolate chips

Glaze

½ cup powdered sugar
⅛ teaspoon nutmeg

⅛ teaspoon cinnamon
2 tablespoons cream

1. Preheat oven to 350°. Grease a 9" x 5" loaf pan.

2. Cream margarine, add sugar and blend in eggs. Combine flour, baking soda, salt, and spices. Add dry ingredients alternately with pumpkin. Fold in nuts and chocolate chips. Pour into loaf pan. Bake for 70 to 80 minutes. Drizzle with glaze and sprinkle with additional chopped nuts.

3. To prepare glaze: Combine powdered sugar, nutmeg, and cinnamon. Blend in cream to desired consistency.

Quick Sally Lunn Bread

Betty Jane Posey
BETTY JANE POSEY GALLERY

This quick version of a southern tradition tastes terrific on its own, or with a bit of fruit compote and whipped topping.

½ cup butter	2 ½ cups flour
1 cup sugar	¼ teaspoon salt
2 eggs, beaten	3 teaspoons baking powder
1 cup milk	

1. Preheat oven to 350°. Grease and flour a 9" x 13" pan.

2. Cream butter and sugar well. Beat in eggs and milk. Sift together flour, salt, and baking powder. Stir into creamed mixture. Bake for 30 minutes.

Annual Squirrel Hunt

Years ago, in the fall of our first year on a North Carolina farm, our neighbor would go out and shoot all the squirrels he could in his yard. It was traditional for him to shoot every squirrel in sight on that particular day. Fattened up from eating chestnuts, the squirrels would be cooked as stew. As a result of this ritual, even with a number of chestnut trees on our property, we didn't have a very large squirrel population around the house.

I used to get all upset and call "come here squirrel" from the other side of the fence, trying to protect them. I soon realized squirrel was a big meat for these folks. All they had to eat most of the time was beans and cornbread.

—Betty Jane Posey
Betty Jane Posey Gallery

Plain Pound Cake

Sue Ownby
E & T WOODCARVINGS

This recipe should be renamed "Plain Delicious Pound Cake." Sue has a gift for good home baking!

2 cups sugar
1 cup margarine, softened
4 eggs
2 cups all purpose flour

1 cup self-rising flour
1 cup milk
1 teaspoon lemon flavoring

1. Preheat oven to 350°. Grease and flour two 9" x 5" loaf pans or a 12" bundt pan.

2. In a large bowl, cream sugar and margarine with electric mixer. Beat until light and fluffy. Stir in eggs, flours, milk, and lemon flavoring. Once mixed, beat on high for 2 minutes.

3. Divide batter into the 2 loaf pans, or bundt pan, and bake for 50 to 65 minutes (depending on size of pan) or until it tests done. Cool on wire rack for 30 minutes before removing from pan. Freezes well.

A good substitute for buttermilk is to put 1 tablespoon vinegar into sweet milk.

—Sue Ownby
E & T Woodcarving

Alewine Pottery

*Y*ou will often find Robert Alewine sitting on a stool behind the counter of his studio "throwing" one of his clay pieces on the potter's wheel. His colorful handpainted works are just as beautiful as they are functional, reflecting his training in both painting and pottery.

In his large showroom on Glades Road you will find bowls, mugs, vases, decorative lamps, complete dinner sets, and beautiful round serving platters just waiting to be used and displayed in your home.

Robert is not the cook in his family, but he apparently can boil water. He says during the March '93 blizzard, he was amazed to discover how much snow you had to melt to get a cup of coffee. His wife Connie does the cooking in their home. Her **Cream Cheese Pound Cake**, just cries out to be served on one of Robert's colorful round serving platters. This exceptionally rich and delicious recipe is sometimes lightened by Connie with the use of low-fat cream cheese and egg substitute.

Cream Cheese Pound Cake

Connie Alewine
ALEWINE POTTERY

I know a number of you will look at this recipe and feel your arteries closing in from all the fat. Think of it as a special occasion cake. It really is worth the mega calories and cholesterol. Do like Robert Alewine does, he balances it off with low-cal meals the next few days.

1 cup margarine, softened	dash of salt
½ cup butter, softened	2 teaspoons vanilla
8 ounces cream cheese, softened	6 large eggs
3 cups sugar	3 cups cake flour

1. Combine margarine, butter, cream cheese, and sugar. Beat well. Add salt and vanilla. Add eggs one at a time beating well after each addition.

2. Add cake flour. Mix well. Pour batter into a greased and floured tube pan. Place in a cold oven. Bake at 275° for 1 ½ to 2 hours. Serves 12 to 15.

Note: When I tested this, I questioned whether 275° was a correct instruction, especially considering it goes into a cold oven. Rest assured it works!

"It's nice being your own boss, but the flipside is that I'm always telling myself to go to work."

—Robert Alewine
Alewine Pottery

The Best Pound Cake

Marsha A. Fountain
GATLIN COUNTY LEATHER

Marsha sent in this recipe (handed down from her maternal grandmother, Nora Gatlin) along with a cute story.

J. E. Gatlin, Marsha's uncle, was five years old in the mid 1920's. He ran across the corn field to a neighbor. The lady had just baked a pound cake. Little J. E. was given a piece, took a bite, and clutched the remainder in his fist. He ran back across the field to his Mom yelling "Bake"! Well, Grandma Gatlin couldn't let a little boy down. She and J. E. went back across the corn field to get this recipe.

1 cup butter, softened or melted	6 eggs
2 cups sugar	2 cups flour
1 teaspoon vanilla	

1. Preheat oven to 350°. Grease and flour a 9" x 5" loaf pan. In a large bowl beat butter and sugar until smooth. Beat in vanilla. Beat in eggs, one at a time, until well blended. Slowly mix in flour.

2. Fill loaf pan ¾ full (there may be leftover batter that may be made into muffins). Bake for 50 to 65 minutes until it tests done with a toothpick. Cool on cake rack. Good with strawberries to peanut butter.

Zucchini Bread

Margaret Seymour
SEYMOUR'S COUNTRY CRAFTS

When your family starts to complain about all the zucchini taking over the garden—let them eat cake. A few bites of this quick bread, and they will be running outside to harvest more for you to bake. This loaf freezes well. In zucchini season stock your freezer with this homemade quick bread.

4 cups shredded zucchini	1 tablespoon ground cinnamon
4 eggs	1 ½ teaspoons salt
2 ½ cups sugar	½ teaspoon baking soda
1 ½ cups vegetable oil	½ teaspoon baking powder
3 cups flour	1 cup chopped pecans

1. Preheat oven to 325°. Grease bottom of two 9" x 5" loaf pans. Grate zucchini and set aside.

2. With electric mixer on low speed beat eggs. Add sugar and oil. Add flour, cinnamon, salt, baking soda, and baking powder. Beat until well blended. Stir in nuts and zucchini. Beat on medium speed for one minute.

3. Pour into prepared pans. Bake for 55 to 65 minutes or until done.

Note: Make sure, when testing if it is done, that a toothpick comes out dry from top center of loaf, otherwise you will have a slightly soggy middle.

The only craft hint I have is "There is no short cut for quality."

—Dick Seymour
Seymour's Country Crafts

Hippensteal's Mountain View

*A*s you turn onto Grassy Branch Road and look up to see Hippensteal's bed and breakfast perched on top of a hill, you just know that the Mountain View Inn is going to live up to its name. The view from the Inn is nothing short of spectacular with the Greenbriar Pinnacle on your left, Mt. Le Conte straight ahead, and Mt. Harrison on your right.

Designed by Vern Hippensteal (one of Gatlinburg's finest watercolor artists), the Inn has been beautifully decorated with loving detail by him and his wife, Lisa. Prints of Vern's own paintings line the walls of the guest rooms and common areas. Each of the eight individually decorated guestrooms have a comfy queen size bed, working fireplace, and private bath with whirlpool tub. The rooms open onto a large wrap-around porch with rocking chairs and the dynamite view.

After your evening's slumber, you are invited down to the diningroom for a delicious homemade breakfast. While in your own home, why not try preparing one of their most popular morning meals, **Sausage Pie** and **Strawberry Bread**.

Strawberry Loaf

Vern Hippensteal
HIPPENSTEAL INN

This companion recipe to **Sausage Pie,** served at the Hippensteal Inn, is their most popular breakfast combination. I have tested this recipe several times, not because it did not work, but because it is so good. The recipe works well using fresh or frozen berries (with or without syrup in frozen berries—you may need to adjust baking time if you use syrup).

2 cups sugar	4 eggs, beaten
3 cups flour	1 ½ cups cooking oil
1 teaspoon baking soda	2 cups frozen strawberries, thawed
1 teaspoon salt	1 ¼ cups chopped pecans
1 tablespoon cinnamon	

1. Preheat oven to 325°. Grease two 9" x 5" loaf pans, or use 3 small loaf pans.

2. In a large bowl, combine sugar, flour, baking soda, salt, and cinnamon. In a separate bowl, beat together eggs and oil. Mix in strawberries.

3. Stir strawberry mixture into dry ingredients and add pecans. Stir just until blended. Pour into prepared pans. Bake for 55 to 65 minutes. Test center of loaf to be sure it is done. Freezes well.

Blueberry Muffins

Joan McGill

GLADES DELI

The texture and taste of these muffins are much like a tea biscuit, a not-too-sweet cross between a biscuit and cake. If you like a touch more sweetness, sprinkle a bit of sugar on top of each one before baking.

1 ¾ cups flour	¾ cup blueberries
2 ½ teaspoons baking powder	1 egg, well beaten
2 tablespoons sugar	½ cup milk
¾ teaspoon salt	½ cup shortening, melted & cooled

1. Preheat oven to 400°. Grease muffin pan.

2. Add flour, baking powder, sugar, and salt together in a mixing bowl. Make a well in center and add blueberries.

3. Combine egg and milk and add to cooled shortening. Add shortening mixture to dry ingredients all at once. Mix well. Fill muffin pans ⅔ full with batter. Bake for 25 minutes, or until lightly browned. Makes 12 muffins.

Mother's Cornmeal Muffins

Martha Powers
OSTEEN & POWERS

This recipe, handed down to Martha from her mother, is quick to prepare. These look as good as they taste when presented in a lovely napkin-lined basket.

1 cup self-rising flour	3 tablespoons sugar
1 cup cornmeal	2 tablespoons shortening
½ teaspoon salt	1 egg, beaten
1 teaspoon baking powder	1 cup milk

1. Preheat oven to 375°. Grease a 12-cup muffin pan.

2. Sift together flour, cornmeal, salt, baking powder, and sugar into a mixing bowl. Cut in shortening.

3. Stir beaten egg and milk into dry ingredients just until blended. Pour into prepared muffin cups and bake for 15 to 20 minutes. Makes 12 muffins. Freezes well.

Pumpkin-Cranberry Muffins

Kathy Shields Guttman

Wonder what to do with the leftover pumpkin in the can after making Helen Vance's **Pumpkin Pie**? These quick and delicious muffins are the answer. You do not have to wait until you have leftover pumpkin, just open up a small can and make a double batch. If you have difficulty finding the dried cranberries, substitute raisins or chocolate chips.

⅔ cup sugar
⅓ cup vegetable oil
1 egg
¾ cup canned pumpkin
1 ¼ cups flour
1 teaspoon baking powder

1 teaspoon baking soda
¼ teaspoon powdered cloves
½ teaspoon cinnamon
¼ teaspoon salt
⅓ cup dried cranberries

1. Preheat oven to 350°. Grease muffin pan.

2. In a medium mixing bowl, beat together sugar and oil. Beat in egg and pumpkin, mixing thoroughly.

3. Combine flour, baking powder, baking soda, cloves, cinnamon, and salt. Stir into pumpkin mixture just until blended. Stir in cranberries. Fill prepared muffin cups ⅔ full. Bake 20 to 25 minutes. Makes 10 to 12 muffins. Freezes well.

Tennessee Orange Raisin Bran Muffins

Vern Hippensteal
Hippensteal Inn

These ambrosial muffins are served at breakfast at the Hippensteal Inn. Organization and timing are key ingredients to preparing a morning feast at a bed and breakfast. Making the muffin batter the night before, saves a little extra time on busy mornings— a good idea that can be used in your own home.

2 large eggs, beaten
1 ½ cups buttermilk
½ cup vegetable oil
½ cup undiluted frozen orange juice, thawed

1 cup sugar
2 ½ cups all purpose flour
1 cup raisin bran cereal
2 ½ teaspoons baking soda
1 teaspoon salt

1. In a mixing bowl, combine eggs, buttermilk, oil, orange juice, and sugar. Mix well. Add flour, cereal, baking soda, and salt. Stir until blended. Refrigerate overnight.

2. Preheat oven to 375°. Grease muffin cups. Spoon batter into cups filling each ⅔ full. Let batter stand for 20 to 30 minutes before placing in oven. Bake for 12 to 14 minutes or until lightly browned. Freezes well. Makes 18 muffins.

Hemlock Falls Rentals

Clarice Maples is an associate member of the Great Smoky Arts & Crafts Community. She and her husband own and operate nightly rental cabins in the Glades. Although not an artisan herself, she is a great admirer of arts and crafts and uses them in her cabins. Her neighbors make them and she buys them.

Chatting with this delightful lady, it is immediately apparent that family is very important to her. She talks lovingly of her husband and children, and with fond memories of her parents. Clarice remembers when, as a young child, her mother packed a lunch in a picnic basket and they spent the day at the Tennessee Valley Fair in Knoxville. She said, "Mother would spread out a checkered tablecloth on the banks of the lake, and we would enjoy our food and play. We spent the whole day there and came home after the fireworks."

Clarice did not say what was packed in their picnic basket, but I would not be surprised if it included some delicious **Apple Fritters** like the ones she now makes for her family.

Apple Fritters

Clarice Maples
HEMLOCK FALLS RENTALS

Clarice says these fritters are good anytime of day, but especially as a morning snack served with apple butter. They are based on a recipe from one of her favorite restaurants, The Apple Barn. For a change of pace, try making these with pears, instead of apples, and add cinnamon to the powdered sugar for coating the fritters.

1 ½ cups flour
1 tablespoon sugar
2 teaspoons baking powder
½ teaspoon salt
2 eggs, beaten
⅔ cup milk

1 tablespoon vegetable oil
3 cups peeled and finely chopped
 apples
vegetable oil for frying
powdered sugar

1. Combine flour, sugar, baking powder, and salt in a bowl. Make a well in center of dry ingredients and add eggs, milk, vegetable oil, and apples. Stir just until moistened.

2. Heat ½" of oil in a large skillet. When oil is hot (see note), drop batter by spoonfuls and cook until golden brown (about 3 to 4 minutes on each side). Drain on paper towel. Roll in powdered sugar. Makes about 2 ½ dozen.

Note: Oil is hot enough when it begins to smoke. If oil becomes too hot, the fritters will brown too quickly and the inside of the fritter will still be wet.

If you run out of coffee filters for your drip coffee maker, use a heavy-weight paper napkin.

—Clarice Maples
Hemlock Falls Nightly Rentals

Apple Carrot Pancakes

Kathy Shields Guttman

Inspired by having carrot pancakes in a favorite restaurant, I came home and created my own version of apple carrot pancakes. Instead of serving these with maple syrup, I melt ½ cup of apricot jam to pour on top.

⅔ cup flour
⅔ cup whole wheat flour
½ teaspoon salt
1 teaspoon baking powder
½ teaspoon baking soda
2 tablespoons honey
1 ¼ cups buttermilk

2 tablespoons vegetable oil
1 egg, beaten
1 small apple, peeled, cored, and
   grated
½ cup grated carrots
vegetable oil for cooking

1. In a mixing bowl, combine flours, salt, baking powder, and baking soda. Add honey, buttermilk, oil, and egg. Mix until smooth. Mix in grated apple and carrots.

2. Pour batter onto a hot, slightly greased griddle or skillet. Cook until bubbles appear on top side. Flip over and brown the other side. Serve immediately or keep warm in low (275°) oven. Makes 14 to 16 pancakes.

"I've met a lot of unusual people coming into the shop. They ask dumb questions and good ones, but I try to make everyone welcome, and they come back every year because of it."

—Gena Lewis
Lewis Family Crafts

Corn Griddle Cakes

THE TEAGUE MILL RESTAURANT

This recipe calls for Teague's stone ground cornmeal. You may substitute regular cornmeal, but it will not have quite the same taste and texture. Before using in a recipe, always sift stone ground cornmeal.

¼ cup flour	1 ¼ cups milk
4 teaspoons baking powder	2 eggs, well beaten
1 ½ cups stone ground cornmeal, sifted	2 tablespoons Teague sorghum molasses
¾ teaspoon salt	1 tablespoon melted butter

1. In a mixing bowl, combine flour, baking powder, cornmeal, and salt. Add milk, eggs, and sorghum molasses (you may substitute with plain molasses or honey). Blend well. Mix in melted butter.

2. Pour batter onto a greased hot griddle. Cook until bubbles appear on top side. Flip and brown the other side. Serve with sorghum molasses and butter. Makes 8 to 10.

Variation: For a savory version of these griddle cakes, omit molasses from batter and add ½ cup fresh or canned corn kernels and ¼ cup fresh chopped cilantro. Serve with tomato salsa. I call these **Cilantro Corn Cakes**.

Whole Wheat Pancakes

THE TEAGUE MILL RESTAURANT

These are a healthy treat for breakfast or lunch. You may dress it up by adding fresh sliced strawberries or grated apple with a little cinnamon.

1 cup Teague whole wheat stone ground flour (unsifted)	1 egg
½ teaspoon salt	1 cup milk
1 teaspoon baking powder	1 tablespoon oil
	1 tablespoon Teague sorghum molasses

1. In a mixing bowl combine whole wheat flour, salt, and baking powder. In a separate bowl, beat egg. Blend in milk and oil. Pour into dry ingredients. Stir. Add sorghum molasses (or honey). Beat until smooth.

2. Pour batter onto a greased hot griddle. Turn pancakes when top side is bubbly and a few bubbles have broken. Flip and brown other side. Makes 8 to 10.

Picture Perfect Pancakes

One of the many fond memories here at the Inn is of an older couple to whom we served our heart shaped pancake, scrambled egg, bacon, and fruit platter. It is a beautiful plate. The pancakes are sprinkled with powdered sugar and served with strawberry butter. When we served the dish, the lady stopped her husband from touching his food. She grabbed her camera and then took several pictures of their breakfast before eating it. This breakfast always gets an "oh, how sweet" response.

—Francis
Hippensteal's Mountain View Inn

CORNBREADS, BISCUITS, & GRITS

Buttermilk Corn Bread

Betty Jane Posey
BETTY JANE POSEY GALLERY

There may be as many different recipes and styles of cornbread, as there are people in the South. Some make cornbread with yellow meal, some with white. There are those who would not think of adding sugar to the batter, and those that prefer it sweet. It is baked in hot iron skillets, glass baking dishes, muffin tins, iron corn stick pans, and deep fried into balls and called hushpuppies.

Betty Jane's old southern family recipe is a fairly traditional cornbread. She bakes it in a hot iron skillet with bacon drippings. This same recipe may be baked in a 9" x 13" pan. If you prefer, grease the skillet, or pan, with vegetable oil.

2 cups self-rising cornmeal	2 eggs
½ cup flour	1 ½ cups buttermilk, approximately
pinch of salt	2 tablespoons bacon drippings, or
2 tablespoons sugar	vegetable oil

1. Preheat oven to 400°. Sift cornmeal, flour, salt, and sugar together and set aside.

2. Beat eggs. Alternately add dry ingredients with buttermilk (add buttermilk until batter is of medium consistency—not thick). Beat well.

3. Heat bacon drippings in iron skillet. Pour batter into hot skillet. Bake for about 35 to 45 minutes until top is golden brown.

The secret to good cornbread is beating well and using hot irons.
—The Teague Mill Restaurant

The Colonel's Corn Bread

Bill Cate
THE COLONEL'S LADY

This original recipe has been in Bill's family for generations. The "secret" ingredient in this recipe is the mayonnaise—Bill uses his own homemade mayonnaise.

2 eggs	2 cups white self-rising cornmeal
1 tablespoon sugar	1 ½ cups buttermilk or sweet milk,
1 cup mayonnaise	approximately

1. Preheat oven to 425°. Grease bottom and sides of iron skillet with vegetable oil or shortening.

2. Beat the eggs and add sugar, mayonnaise, cornmeal, and buttermilk (add buttermilk until batter is of medium consistency). Beat until well blended.

3. Pour batter into greased skillet. Bake for 25 to 35 minutes until golden brown.

To get that extra sparkle when cleaning glass, add a little distilled vinegar to the solution.

—Bill Cate
Colonel's Lady

Mexican Cornbread

Peggy Bailey
WHISPERING PINES

Just before you are finished baking Peggy's cornbread, step outside for a moment. When you re-enter your home, the aroma coming out of your kitchen will set your taste buds on fire with anticipation. If you are worried the hot peppers might set your mouth on fire, adjust the quantity and intensity of the peppers.

1 large onion, grated
1 can cream style corn (14 ounces)
3 eggs
3 small hot peppers, seeded and
   chopped

1 small sweet pepper, seeded and
   chopped
½ cup vegetable oil
1 ½ cups self-rising cornmeal
1 ½ to 2 cups grated cheddar cheese

1. Preheat oven to 350°. Generously grease black iron skillet (or a 7" x 11" baking dish) with oil.

2. Mix grated onion with corn, eggs, peppers, vegetable oil, and cornmeal. Beat thoroughly.

3. Heat greased skillet in oven. Pour ½ batter into hot skillet. Sprinkle all but ½ cup of cheese on top of batter. Pour remaining batter on top. Sprinkle remaining cheese on top and bake for 30 to 35 minutes until golden brown.

Note: Using a food processor makes preparing this recipe a snap. Grate the cheese and set aside. Grate the onion and add the remaining ingredients. Process for 5 to 8 seconds and it is ready to bake.

Sweet Corn Bread

Buckhorn Inn

The sweet taste and moist texture of this cornbread goes great as a side dish with dinner, a muffin for breakfast, a great snack for a lunchbox, and a simple dessert.

½ cup butter
1 cup sugar
2 eggs
1 cup yellow cornmeal

1 ½ cups flour
2 teaspoons baking powder
½ teaspoon salt
1 ½ cups milk

1. Preheat oven to 375°. Grease an 8" square pan or a 12-cup muffin pan.

2. In a mixing bowl, cream together the butter and sugar. Add the eggs, beating well, then add cornmeal. Sift the flour with baking powder and salt. Stir in alternately with the milk.

3. Pour into square pan. Bake for 30 to 35 minutes, or, if using muffin pan, bake for 15 to 20 minutes.

The Teague Mill

Whenen you ask Gatlinburg residents about their favorite restaurants in the area, time and again they will suggest Teague's Creekside Dining and the Teague Mill.

Both locations have consistently good food, friendly service, and unique settings. The Creekside location (a long narrow screen-porch type of structure) sits right on top of Dudley Creek and has a red tin roof with water running off of it. Even on the hottest of days, with water running over and under this restaurant, you are assured of a cool refreshing dining atmosphere. Fresh rainbow trout, prime rib, mesquite broiled chicken, and lasagna are a few of their specialties.

Teague Mill Restaurant is a big hit with families. It has a working water-powered gristmill, antique smokehouse, and general store; and if you like, you may catch your own fish in their trout pond. In addition to the fresh rainbow trout, their menu includes hickory smoked barbecued rib and chicken dinners, country ham, and crisp tender hushpuppies made from their own stone ground cornmeal. Teague has a mail order catalogue for their products for those people like myself who go back home and cannot find grits (stone ground or otherwise) anywhere in town.

The recipes they have contributed to this book are best with stone ground grits, whole wheat flour, and cornmeal, but you may substitute with a regular commercial product.

Teague's Cornbread

THE TEAGUE MILL RESTAURANT

The special part of this recipe is using Teague's stone ground cornmeal.

1 cup plus 2 tablespoons stone
    ground cornmeal, sifted
½ cup flour
½ teaspoon salt
½ teaspoon baking soda

½ teaspoon baking powder
1 egg, well beaten
2 tablespoons oil or bacon drippings
1 cup buttermilk

1. Preheat oven to 425°. Grease a medium size iron skillet.

2. In a mixing bowl combine cornmeal, flour, salt, baking soda, and baking powder. Beat in egg, oil, and buttermilk.

3. Heat greased iron skillet until hot enough to sizzle. Pour in batter and bake for 20 minutes until brown.

Note: Always sift a stone ground cornmeal before using it in a recipe. If you are unable to FIND stone ground cornmeal in your area, you may order it from Teague's. Their address is listed in the appendix.

Variation: To make **Corn Sticks**, use the above recipe and fill well greased and heated corn stick iron pans with batter ½ full. Bake at 450° for 10 minutes.

"Rumour has it that the real reason the Civil War started is because some Yankee put sugar in the cornbread."

—Anonymous

Teague's Hushpuppies

THE TEAGUE MILL RESTAURANT

Using stone ground cornmeal makes the texture of these hushpuppies light and tender. These go great as a side dish with a hearty bowl of soup, or some southern fried chicken.

1 cup sifted stone ground cornmeal	¾ to 1 cup milk
½ cup flour	pinch of sugar
1 teaspoon salt	1 small chopped onion
2 teaspoons baking powder	1 tablespoon melted shortening
1 egg, well beaten	vegetable oil or shortening for frying

1. In a mixing bowl, sift together cornmeal, flour, salt, and baking powder. Add egg, milk (enough to make a medium thick batter), sugar, and onion. Add shortening and mix batter thoroughly.

2. Heat vegetable oil or shortening in deep-fryer (you may use a heavy saucepan, or even a wok for frying) to 325°. Drop batter from tablespoon (½ full) into hot fat. Cook for 2 to 3 minutes until golden brown.

Note: Each time before lifting batter with tablespoon, dip spoon in cold water.

Always sift out the hulls in stone ground cornmeal before using in a recipe.
—The Teague Mill Restaurant

Hushpuppies

Carl Fogliani
COSBY HILLPEOPLE CRAFTS

Hushpuppies are deep-fried cornbread balls. Rumor has it that cowpokes, out on the range, would fry up a batch of these balls and toss them to their dogs to keep them from howling.

Carl's own recipe for hushpuppies are crisp on the outside and steaming hot and tender inside. When Carl makes these for his family, he does not measure the ingredients, he just throws them together until the consistency and quantity of the batter looks right. He serves these as a side dish with his Batter Fried Fish.

3 cups self-rising cornmeal	1 ¾ to 2 cups buttermilk
3 eggs	1 medium onion, chopped
¼ teaspoon garlic powder	vegetable shortening or oil for frying

1. In a large bowl, whisk together the cornmeal, eggs, garlic powder, buttermilk, and onion. Beat with a whisk until thoroughly blended.

2. In a deep fryer, heat oil to 350°. Use a teaspoon to drop batter into hot oil. Cook for 1 to 1½ minutes. Break one open to test (the batter should be fully cooked, not wet in the middle). Drain on a paper towel. Keep warm in oven while frying remaining batter.

"I don't hike. If it is some place my truck can't get to, then I don't need to be there."
—Carl Fogliani
Crosby Hillpeople Crafts

Indian Bread

Betty Jane Posey
BETTY JANE POSEY GALLERY

You may make these using regular cornmeal, but they are really special made with a stone ground cornmeal. Betty Jane bakes these in miniature muffin tins, however, you may use standard muffin tins.

¾ cup stone ground cornmeal   3 eggs, well beaten
1 cup hot milk   ¼ teaspoon salt

1. Preheat oven to 400°. Grease muffin tin.

2. In a saucepan, stir cornmeal into hot milk until it thickens. Mix in eggs and salt. Fill muffin cups ¾ full and bake for 30 minutes. Serve immediately.

An Unforgettable Thanksgiving Dinner

While working at the University of Georgia Veterinary School as a young lab technician, we had a project doing research on turkeys. We had 24 turkeys—12 of them as controls without disease and 12 with diseases. When we got to the end of the project, the diseased turkeys were put to sleep. The other 12 were perfectly fine. My boss said "You can have those 12 turkeys if you kill them." When I asked how, he said "Use an anesthetic, it is the humane way to do it." I killed all 12.

For the first turkey, I had to recollect a vague memory from my childhood on how to defeather. I got through that alright, but no one ever told me about gutting the turkey before cooking it. We ended up throwing that one out. For the second turkey, we invited friends over for a big Thanksgiving dinner. We sat down to eat, and when we got up, nobody could walk straight. No one bothered to mention that if you inject anesthetic it stays in the turkey's tissue. We all walked around doped up for two days!

—Betty Jane Posey
Betty Jane Posey Gallery

Biscuits

Charlotte Boles
WHISPERING PINES WOODCRAFTS

What could be more southern than biscuits? Whether you choose to make the "whop" variety, or biscuits from scratch, they are a welcome addition to any meal. Each southern family has their own special recipe. Some are light in texture, and some are more dense and crisp. Charlotte's family recipe falls into the latter category.

2 cups sifted self-rising flour   **⅔ cup milk**
3 tablespoon shortening

1. Preheat oven to 450°. Sift flour first and then measure 2 cups into a mixing bowl. Cut shortening into flour until the size of coarse crumbs. Add milk and mix with fork to make a soft dough.

2. Remove dough and place on lightly floured board. Knead for 10 to 12 strokes. Roll ½" thick. Dip biscuit cutter into flour and cut straight down without twisting. Place biscuits touching one another on lightly greased baking pan. Bake for 10 to 12 minutes.

To remove stain from Tupperware, soak in solution of one Efferdent tablet per two cups of water overnight. This does not leave the aftertaste that bleach does.

—Annetta Hendrickson
Leather Works

Joan's Biscuits

Joan McGill
GLADES DELI

Joan's biscuits fall into the light category. Her advice, "for best biscuits always dough as little as possible." Working the dough too much will toughen the biscuits. Always work with floured hands and floured board when kneading dough.

2 cups self-rising flour
¾ cup vegetable shortening

⅔ to ¾ cup buttermilk

1. Preheat oven to 425°. Measure flour into bowl and cut in shortening until the size of coarse crumbs.

2. Blend in enough milk with fork until dough forms and follows fork around bowl (see note). Remove from bowl. Gently knead on floured surface for 10 to 14 strokes. Roll ½" thick. Dip floured biscuit cutter into flour and cut straight down without twisting.

3. Place biscuits next to each other on ungreased baking sheet. Do not leave space between them. Bake for 12 to 16 minutes until golden brown.

Note: Too much milk makes dough too sticky to handle. Not enough milk makes biscuits dry.

Milkless Biscuits

Pat Wills
The Leather Works

Pat's eyes light up when he talks about the delicious biscuits his wife makes. Without milk, they are perfect for those who are lactose intolerant. When making biscuits, she does not measure flour. She puts some in a large bowl and uses as much as necessary.

self-rising flour (about 3 cups)	1 egg
2 tablespoons vegetable shortening	1 cup water
1 tablespoon margarine, melted	

1. In a large bowl of self-rising flour, whip shortening, margarine, egg, and water with fingers (using fingers makes biscuits fluffy) to blend. Whip lightly mixed ingredients into flour until large moist ball forms. Knead a few times with floured hands.

2. Turn ball out on a baking sheet with melted margarine. Tear off dough to form balls a little larger than a golf ball. Flatten with floured hands. Place on baking sheet. Biscuits should be touching each other. Bake in a preheated 400° oven for 12 to 15 minutes until golden. Makes 10 to 12 biscuits.

Whole Wheat Biscuits

The Teague Mill Restaurant

My husband is not a fan of biscuits, but he has been a good sport in taste-testing all the biscuits I've made for this book. The only one he really liked was this whole wheat biscuit. Its different taste and texture is a nice change from regular white flour biscuits.

1 cup stone ground whole wheat
    flour (unsifted)
1 cup flour
3 teaspoons baking powder

¾ teaspoon salt
¼ cup shortening
⅔ to ¾ cup milk

1. Preheat oven to 450°. In a mixing bowl, combine whole wheat flour, all-purpose flour, baking powder, and salt. Cut in shortening until size of coarse crumbs.

2. Make a well in dry ingredients and add milk all at once. Stir quickly with fork until dough follows fork around bowl. Remove dough and place on lightly floured surface. Knead gently 10–12 strokes.

3. Roll or pat dough ½" thick. Dip biscuit cutter in flour and cut straight down, no twisting. Place together (biscuits touching one another) on ungreased baking sheet. Bake for 12-15 minutes. Makes 16 biscuits.

Gravy and sauces can be made without fat or oil. Mix flour or cornstarch with cold water and cook slowly until thick. For brown gravy, use Kitchen Bouquet (a vegetarian browning agent) for color, and spice accordingly.

—Gena Lewis
Lewis Family Crafts

Popovers

Betty Jane Posey
BETTY JANE POSEY GALLERY

This is Betty Jane's favorite bread recipe. These Yorkshire Pudding style popovers melt in your mouth, and the best part is, they are easy. Try making these the next time you serve roast beef, or bake up a batch to enjoy with soup for a simple dinner.

2 eggs	1 teaspoon salt
1 cup milk	2 tablespoons butter, divided into ½
1 cup flour	teaspoons

1. In a blender, mix eggs, milk, flour, and salt until smooth. Refrigerate until ready to bake.

2. Preheat oven to 425°. Grease muffin pan (twelve 2 ½" cups). Place ½ teaspoon butter in each cup. Place in oven until butter melts and sizzles.

3. Remove pan from oven. Pour batter into cups, filling ⅔ full. Return to oven for 25 to 30 minutes until puffed and brown. Do not open oven to peek while baking. Serve immediately.

"We bought my wife's old home place in 1982 and started to build our house. Believe it or not, we are almost finished. Located up in the mountains near the North Carolina line, it borders the Great Smoky National Park. If you get down this way, be sure to stop in and see us at our studio. But, if there's about three inches of snow, I'll have about 12 inches at my place—so don't look for me that day. I'll be in my Lazy Boy in front of the fireplace."

—Carl Fogliani
Cosby Hillpeople Crafts

G. Webb Gallery

*R*ight on the corner of Glades and Buckhorn is a turn-of-the-century board and batten house framed on the outside by wildflower gardens and majestic hemlock trees. This old homeplace-turned-art gallery houses G. Webb's original watercolors, prints, and drawings. His work focuses on the heritage of the Smoky Mountains, its landscapes, landmarks, florals, and people.

G's wife Vicki says "He is a true artist—put him in an empty room and he would still come out with a beautiful painting." However, an empty room is not where he likes to paint. He loves painting on location: amongst the huge boulders of the Greenbrier River, up on top of Mt. Le Conte, and on the shores of Seaside, Florida where his family vacations in May.

Continually growing and developing interests, G. creates and cultivates everything from paintings and flower gardens, to butterflies and lady bugs. Recently he plunged into the world of publishing by illustrating the mountain life poems and short stories of Ron Evans in a collaborative book entitled *When The Leaves Have Fallen.*

In addition to other areas, G's creativity flourishes in the kitchen. His recipes for **Jumbalaya** and **Southern Railroad Ties** shows his talent for producing food that is both fun and delicious!

Southern Railroad Ties

G. Webb

G. WEBB GALLERY

Always the artist, it seems G. likes to create form with his food. These biscuits depicting railroad ties are fun, fast, and delicious. For a trip down a different track, before baking, try sprinkling these with Parmesan cheese and/or your favorite herbs.

1 cup packaged biscuit mix　　　　　　**¼ cup melted margarine, divided**
⅓ cup milk

1. Preheat oven to 450°. Place biscuit mix in a mixing bowl. Add milk all at once. Stir with fork into a soft dough. Knead dough 8 to 10 times on floured board.

2. Shape dough into a railroad track 12" long by 3" to 4" wide. Create railroad ties by making a cut (do not cut all the way through dough) every ¾" along the track. Create rails by gently marking a line in dough about ½" along both sides of track.

3. Pour ½ of melted margarine on baking sheet. Place dough on top of margarine and pour remainder of margarine on top of dough. Bake for 10 to 15 minutes. Pass around plate and let everyone break off a tie!

"Some of my fondest food memories are eating my Grandma Webb's homemade biscuits, and my wife's too!"

—G. Webb
G. Webb Gallery

Shucks Y'All

*E*leanor Hopf's colorful handcrafted flowers, wreaths, wall hangings, arrangements, and dolls made of cornshucks are attractively displayed in shared space with Adoughable Things by Nancy. In a separate adjoining room Eleanor displays and sells quilts and braided rugs.

Eleanor's personality is as colorful as the name of her store and the cornshucks she creates. If this book were wired for sight and sound, you would be able to hear and see her tell a story that leaves you doubled over with laughter. With her hearty southern accent, and moving around the room with arms up and body hunched over, she describes the time her puppies were "yapping away" outside. She went out to discover a "big ole bear!" It chased her around a tree until she escaped back to the house and telephoned Daddy to the rescue. The story ends with Daddy driving up in his Cadillac and stomping up the path with shotgun at the ready.

It's thanks to Eleanor's descriptive way with words, that I finally came up with a title for this book. When she described to me, just what a "Whop Biscuit" is, I knew this had to be part of the book's title. Eleanor's "Whop Biscuits" epitomizes the essence of this book, namely to show the diversity of style and depth of personality of the arts and crafts community.

"Whop Biscuits"

Eleanor Hopf
Shucks Y'All

When I asked Eleanor if she had any biscuit recipes, she replied "Well, I just make 'Whop Biscuits.' I buy a can of those refrigerated biscuits from the store, whop the can on the edge of the counter, and place the biscuits in the pan!"

I couldn't stop laughing. I had heard of Angel Biscuits and Cat Head Biscuits, but never Whop Biscuits. What a great name for a recipe. What a great name for a book!

If the truth be known, the refrigerated package dough is what a lot of us use these days. Biscuits are tricky to make, but **Whop Biscuits** are a success every time. I've experimented with a few variations of "Whop Biscuits," here are a few ideas to try:

- Dip each biscuit in melted butter and sprinkle with Parmesan cheese, dried parsley, and paprika.
- Slice each biscuit in the middle and insert a small piece of cheddar cheese, brush top with butter and sprinkle with dried basil and oregano.
- Press the top and sides of each biscuit in oat bran cereal before baking (optional—you may spray biscuits with cooking spray before coating them with cereal).
- Coat the top of each biscuit with butter-flavored cooking spray and then dip into a mixture of chili powder, dill weed, and garlic powder.

Caramel Rolls Made Easy

Maria Holloway
Holloway's Country Home

I was thrilled when Maria sent me this recipe. I knew it would fit in the "Whop Biscuit" section. These rolls are easy and fun to make and are finger-licking good. For a small group, cut the recipe in half; or make the whole amount and freeze some for later.

4 cans refrigerated biscuits (10 biscuit size)
¾ cup margarine

1 ½ cups firm packed brown sugar
3 tablespoons water
¾ cup crushed walnuts

1. Generously grease 26 muffin cups. Whop open package and cut each biscuit in half. Roll each half into a ball and place 3 balls in each muffin cup.

2. Preheat oven to 350° while preparing sauce. In a saucepan, melt margarine. Add brown sugar. Stir until melted. Add water and crushed walnuts. Heat until foamy, stirring frequently. Be careful not to burn sauce. Pour heaping tablespoon onto each biscuit cup.

3. Bake for 15 minutes. Cool for 2 minutes. Remove from pan and place on wax paper. Heat remaining sauce and spoon some over each roll. Makes 26.

Household tip—Have a maid if possible, or at least a husband who doesn't mind doing dishes and putting out the trash.

—Maria Holloway
Holloway's Country Home

Cooked Cheese Grits

Betty Jane Posey
BETTY JANE POSEY GALLERY

When Betty Jane and Cecil ran their restaurant years ago, they served a side of grits with each breakfast. Those who never had grits before, wanted to know what they were and where to buy them.

Grits are amazingly versatile. They may be used as a morning cereal, a luncheon casserole, a fried side dish for supper, or made into a creamy dessert (check the recipe for **Grits à la Colonel**).

3 cups water
1 ½ cups grits (quick cook, not instant)
⅓ stick margarine or butter

½ cup milk or evaporated milk
1 cup grated cheese, Swiss or cheddar
salt and pepper

1. In a saucepan, bring water to a boil. Add grits all at once, stirring immediately. Turn down heat to low and cook about 5 minutes, stirring frequently.

2. Add margarine, milk, and cheese. Stir well and continue cooking until desired thickness. Sprinkle with salt and pepper. Grits should be thick enough to eat with a fork, not a spoon.

"I love to visit Cliff Tops on Mt. Le Conte—Jungle Brook, after a summer rain—Cades Cove anytime—Clingman's Dome before a storm—Newfound Gap at midnight to count stars—Round Bottom Road for a country drive—Parson's Branch when you want to feel lost—Greggory's Bald when you're feeling super human."

—Charlotte Boles
Whispering Pines

Colonel's Lady

*R*eminiscent of an old English country inn, the Colonel's Lady is decorated with antiques, original paintings, and objects of art from around the world. Each of the eight guest rooms and suites are adorned with period furniture and named after English people or places. Their London Bridge Room has a bedroom and sitting area with French doors opening onto a veranda and bridge leading to a private treehouse with a hot tub and panoramic mountain view.

This beautiful bed-and-breakfast inn is a popular spot for honey-mooners. They usually book their first anniversary before leaving for home. Indeed, they have had over 45 weddings at the inn. Most book their first anniversary before they leave, requesting their same suite. They have even had honeymoon couples who arrange to stay 14 nights at the inn, spending two nights in each of seven different rooms.

Bill and Anita Cate have been proprietors of the Colonel's Lady since May 1993. Bill is proud of the food they serve for breakfast at the inn. He says it is a good part of what keeps people coming back season after season, year after year. Try his **Grits à la Colonel** and I think you will understand why they keep returning.

Grits à la Colonel

Bill Cate
Colonel's Lady

Rich and creamy, these grits would be great for dessert or Sunday brunch. You may use quick grits for this recipe or stone ground grits. Stone ground takes a little longer, but the taste and texture is worth it.

For the younger folks having breakfast at the Inn, and for those who do not wish to consume alcohol, they substitute vanilla for Amaretto, and call it **Grits à la Chloe** (named after the owner's daughter).

cooked grits (enough for 6 servings)	1 ounce heavy whipping cream
¼ cup butter	½ ounce Amaretto liqueur
¼ cup sugar	

1. Prepare grits according to package directions. Add butter, sugar, and cream. Whip with whisk until creamy.

2. Dish hot grits into a bowl and drizzle Amaretto on top. Serve immediately.

Variation: To make **Grits à la Canadienne**, substitute real maple syrup for Amaretto.

Fried Grits

Betty Jane Posey
BETTY JANE POSEY GALLERY

Leftover grits, plain, cheese, or otherwise, may be used for fried grits. They are so good, you may want to make some just for frying. Simply cook grits, pour in a loaf pan, and cut into slices when cold and firm.

cold cooked grits, sliced
1 egg, beaten

vegetable oil or margarine

1. Dip sliced grits into egg and fry in oil or margarine until golden brown. Sprinkle with salt and pepper or serve with syrup for a sweet treat.

Variation: To make **Italian Style Fried Grits**, dip cold grits slices into egg mixture, coat with Italian bread crumbs mixed with Parmesan Cheese. Fry in oil.

For **Cinnamon Toast Grits** dip cold slices into egg, fry in margarine, and sprinkle with sugar and cinnamon.

Hashbrown Grits

Kathy Shields Guttman

This is one of my favorite ways to serve grits to unsuspecting dinner guests. It looks like hash brown potatoes, but one bite tells you it is not. The uninitiated guest has just been introduced to grits and loves them.

cold cooked grits
oil and margarine for frying

1 onion, chopped
salt and pepper

1. Slice and dice cold grits into 1" pieces. Heat a combination of oil and margarine in large skillet on medium high heat. Add chopped onion and diced grits.

2. Stir and turn frequently with spatula to prevent sticking and burning. Fry until a crisp golden brown, about 20 minutes. Sprinkle with salt and pepper.

MEATS,
POULTRY, & FISH

Buckhorn Inn

Visiting the Buckhorn Inn is like staying overnight with one of your favorite rich relatives. The friendly staff (managed by innkeepers John and Connie Burns) make you feel like a welcomed and pampered guest in elegant comfortable surroundings. Its sitting room, complete with wall to wall bookshelves, grand piano, stone fireplace, and picture windows (with magnificent views of Mt. LeConte), sets the tone for a relaxed visit in this special place.

The five guest rooms at the Inn are tastefully furnished with antiques and artwork collected by its owner Rachael Young. There is also a unique bedroom built in Buckhorn's original water-tower. Nestled in woodlands are four cottages and two guest houses. This is all set amongst 35 acres of forest, meadows, flower gardens, a pond, and walkways including a self-guided nature trail.

Each morning guests at the Inn are treated to a hearty breakfast prepared by one of its two professional chefs. Most evenings, both guests at the Inn and townspeople may make reservations to enjoy one of their candlelight six-course gourmet dinners, a taste experience I highly recommend. John Burns was kind enough to share several of their recipes for this book. One of my favorites is the **Marinated Beef Tenderloin**; this, along with their **Mud Pie** for dessert, makes for a truly memorable meal.

Marinated Beef Tenderloin

Buckhorn Inn

This marinade is fantastic! My family liked it so much, we used the same marinade recipe to barbecue chuck steaks the following week. My budget does not allow for beef tenderloin on a regular basis.

Forget the old rule of serving red wine with beef. The combination of hot sauce and soy sauce in the marinade makes it difficult to match with a red wine. My local wine connoisseur suggested serving it with cold beer or a medium sweet white wine such as Gewurztraminer or German Riesling. The cold beer worked best!

5 to 6 pound beef tenderloin	1 tablespoon cracked black pepper
1 cup soy sauce	2 teaspoons hot sauce
1 cup red wine	1 teaspoon thyme
½ cup olive oil	3 bay leaves
3 large cloves garlic	

1. Place tenderloin in a non-metalic baking pan. In a large bowl combine the soy sauce, red wine, olive oil, garlic, black pepper, hot sauce, thyme, and bay leaves. Mix well and pour over the tenderloin. Cover and marinate in the refrigerator for 6 to 10 hours.

2. Drain and reserve marinade. Roast tenderloin in a 350° oven for 1 hour and 15 minutes or until meat thermometer registers 140° for medium rare. Slice and serve with heated reserved marinade.

According to The University of Wisconsin's Madison Food Research Institute, wood cutting boards are safer than plastic.

—Ross Markley
Woodturner & Baskets

Mac's Beef & Gravy

Mac McDonell
GEMSTONE

Mac's family recipe for roast beef has a smooth spicy gravy. Serve with mash potatoes, or plain steamed rice, to take advantage of the gravy. Try adding fresh sliced mushrooms during the last 10 minutes of simmering the gravy. For a great finish to this meal, serve Mac's **Key Lime Pie**.

Roast

> 3 pound rump roast or sirloin tip
> 1 tablespoon salt
> ½ teaspoon pepper

> ½ teaspoon fresh or powdered garlic
> 1 teaspoon sugar

Gravy

> 3 tablespoons oil (fat from beef, or vegetable oil)
> 1 ½ to 2 tablespoons flour

> 1 cup water
> 1 cup meat juice (drippings from beef)

1. Place roast on a double layer of aluminum foil. Rub roast liberally with salt, pepper, garlic, and sugar. Wrap foil around roast making sure it is tightly sealed.

2. Roast at 400° for 1 to 2 hours; 1 hour for rare, 1 ¼ for medium, 2 hours for well done. Open and pour all juice into a gravy separator to separate oil and juice. Rewrap meat in foil to keep warm while making gravy.

3. To prepare gravy, heat oil in frying pan. Add enough flour to thicken oil. Stir until brown. Add water and meat juice. Stir and simmer for about 15 minutes. Taste and, if necessary, adjust seasonings.

"I chuckle to myself when visitors tell me how lucky we are to be doing our craft, and that they can't because 'they have to work for a living'!"

—Susan McDonell
Gemstone

Nina's Brisket

Kathy Shields Guttman

This is a special recipe, given to me by a very special person, Nina Globus Schwartz. Every Passover, Nina would bring her famous brisket for dinner. I would try to make it during the year with her recipe, but my family insisted Nina's was better, and it was! During the writing of this cookbook, Nina suddenly passed away. She will be missed, but not forgotten.

Her recipe for brisket is moist and tender. The secret to this is in the long slow cooking overnight, and removing the brisket from its gravy while cooling completely before slicing.

6 large carrots, sliced	**paprika**
5 to 6 pound brisket of beef	**1 cup water**
1 package dry onion soup mix	

1. This cooks in a slow oven overnight. Preheat oven to 175°. Place sliced carrots in the bottom of a large roasting pan. Rub brisket with onion soup mix on both sides of meat. Place brisket, fat side up, on top of carrots in roaster. Sprinkle generously with paprika. Put water in pan. Cover well with aluminum foil.

2. About 10:00 p.m. place prepared brisket in 175° oven. In the morning, remove foil and check to make sure there are pan juices, if not add some water. Replace foil on top of roaster and turn oven heat up to 325° and roast for 1 hour.

3. Remove brisket from gravy and wrap tightly in aluminum foil. Allow to cool completely and then slice against the grain into ¼" slices. To serve, reheat slices in gravy and carrots. Serve with steamed rice or mashed potatoes to take advantage of the gravy.

To take the wild taste out of meat, put in four or five rutabagas and boil. After boiling wild meat with rutabagas, remove them. They absorb the gamey flavor. If you want rutabagas in recipe, put fresh ones in second boiling.

—Mac McDonell
Gemstone

Beef Burgundy

Frances Fox
FIBER CREATIONS

A quick version of an old classic, Frances likes to make this in a slow cooker (crockpot). It can also be easily made by browning the beef in a Dutch oven and baking it, covered, in a 325° oven. If baking in the oven, check to see if you need to add more wine or water to keep the sauce from drying out.

1 ½ pounds sirloin tip, cut in bite size pieces
1 tablespoon vegetable oil
1 can golden mushroom soup
¼ cup Burgundy
2 tablespoons chopped parsley
⅛ teaspoon pepper

12 pearl onions (fresh, or canned and drained)
2 cups sliced fresh mushrooms
12 ounce package wide egg noodles
6 slices bacon, cooked and crumbled
parsley for garnish

1. Brown meat quickly in oil over high heat in crockpot, or in a Dutch oven. Add canned soup, Burgundy, parsley, pepper, onions, and mushrooms. Turn heat to low and cook for at least 1 ½ hours.

2. Prepare egg noodles according to package directions. Serve Beef Burgundy over noodles. Garnish with crumbled bacon and parsley.

When grilling fresh fish, top with chopped fennel leaves.

—Frances Fox
Fiber Creations

Beef Stew

Betty Jane Posey
Betty Jane Posey Gallery

It is winter and it is cold outside. You're getting tired of the short days and long nights. You need something to comfort and warm you. Betty Jane's Beef Stew is just the ticket!

3 to 4 pound chuck or shoulder roast
1 tablespoon Kitchen Bouquet
¼ cup water
salt and pepper
all purpose flour (about ½ cup)
¼ cup vegetable oil
2 cans beef consomme

¼ cup Burgundy wine
3 onions, chopped
2 celery stalks, chopped
4 carrots, sliced
6 to 8 potatoes, cut in 1" cubes
1 can sliced mushrooms (or 8 ounces fresh)

1. Cut meat into 1 inch cubes. In a large bowl, mix Kitchen Bouquet with water. Salt and pepper beef. Allow to soak in Kitchen Bouquet for at least 30 minutes. Dredge soaked beef in flour and set aside.

2. In a large Dutch oven, heat oil until very hot. Brown cubes of meat in batches. After browned, add consomme and wine. Add onions, celery, carrots, potatoes, and mushrooms.

3. Cover pot and place in oven. Roast at 325° for 1 ½ hours.

A carving knife has to be sharp. After sharpening, you have to hone your blade. You can do this with a good piece of leather and honing compound. Draw the blade backwards across the leather several times. Doing it backwards prevents cutting up the leather.

—Otto Preske
Otto Preske—Artist in Wood

Buie Pottery

*B*uie Pottery is the kind of place you walk into and start "oohing and aahing" at each piece of colorfully handcrafted pottery. The colors Buie Boling uses on her functional, as well as decorative, pieces are vibrant and unique.

Like the colors she uses, Buie may also be described as vibrant and unique. In the slower winter season, you might find her away from the studio performing and touring with a steel drum band.

She frequently finds herself in unusual situations. One time she offered to deliver newsletters to save the GSACC some postage. She ended up delivering 73 newsletters over 12 miles of side roads on her motorcycle. That event instantly created the legend of the "Buie (a.k.a. Pony) Express."

Buie enjoys "going to friends birthday parties in the Chimneys Picnic Area and cooking out for 20 or so wild (and crazy by nature) artists and crafters. They all like telling tall tales, and playing guitar long into the night." Next time you are asked to bring a dish to a party, why not take Buie's **Porcupine Balls**, a unique tasty recipe, and a big plate of her **Old English Tea Cakes** for dessert.

Porcupine Balls

Buie Boling
Buie Pottery

These spikey little balls are fun and easy to make, not to mention, delicious to eat. Buie says, "This is a recipe from my grandmother (and a truly wonderful person besides), Margaret McConnaughey."

½ cup uncooked rice	2 tablespoons oil
1 pound ground beef	1 can condensed tomato soup
1 ½ teaspoons salt	1 soup can hot water
¼ teaspoon pepper	egg and/or ketchup, optional
2 tablespoons minced onion	

1. In a large mixing bowl, combine rice, beef, salt, pepper, and onion into balls. Heat oil in frying pan and brown meatballs. Pour off some of the fat.

2. Add soup and water to meatballs. Cover and cook over medium low heat for 1 hour until rice is tender. Check after 30 minutes, you may need to add extra water.

Note: If you use an extra-lean ground beef, you may want to add an egg and/or a couple of tablespoons of ketchup to the meat mixture before forming into balls (it makes the balls a little more moist inside).

"I was one of the very few people in high school that knew what I wanted to do with my life, and one of the even fewer people who didn't change majors in College. I graduated in 1986 from The University of Tennessee with a Bachelor of Fine Arts, with honors, concentrating in ceramics (pottery to the rest of the world). I actually started my business in Gatlinburg before I graduated at age 21. Blind faith goes a long way, and I'm still here."

—Buie Boling
Buie Pottery

Stuffed Meat Loaf

Gil Knier
HERITAGE ARTS

Be warned, once you try Gil's meatloaf, you may never want to go back to your old favorite recipe for this time-honored comfort food. Gil serves this with baked potatoes, green vegetables, and fruit salad.

Meatloaf Mixture

2 pounds lean hamburger
1 cup bread crumbs
2 eggs, beaten
¼ teaspoon garlic powder

½ teaspoon salt
¼ teaspoon pepper
½ cup chili sauce

Stuffing Mixture

1 cup mushrooms, coarsely chopped
¾ cup onions, chopped
1 tablespoon chopped chives
1 cup chopped mild salami or ham

¾ cup grated Swiss or mozzarella cheese
¼ cup sliced olives, optional
¼ cup chopped green peppers, optional

1. Meatloaf mixture: In a large mixing bowl combine hamburger, bread crumbs, eggs, garlic powder, salt, pepper, and chili sauce. Knead mixture well. Spread it on a bread board or wax paper. Shape into a 9" square.

2. Stuffing mixture: In a bowl, combine mushrooms, onions, chives, salami, cheese, olives, and green peppers. Place mixture in middle of the meat. Fold meat into a loaf to enclose the stuffing. Pinch all seams together well, including the ends.

3. Put loaf in greased 9" x 5" loaf pan. Bake at 350° for 1 hour. Remove and let set 10 minutes before serving.

Hamburger Pie

Nancy Hopf
ADOUGHABLE THINGS BY NANCY

Serve this with mashed potatoes and green peas for a quick easy meal for family, or a casual get-together with friends. This is a great recipe to take to a pot-luck supper.

2 pounds ground beef
½ cup chopped onion
1 cup chopped celery
½ cup chopped green pepper
2 cans tomato soup

½ teaspoon garlic powder
1 ½ teaspoons Worcestershire sauce
dash pepper
2 unbaked pie shells
grated cheese, optional

1. Preheat oven to 400°. Brown meat and drain grease. Add onion, celery, and green pepper. Saute for a few minutes. Add tomato soup, garlic powder, Worcestershire sauce, and pepper. Stir and cook for 5 minutes.

2. Divide meat mixture into 2 empty pie tins. Cover meat with pie crusts. Bake for 15 minutes. Turn each pie onto a plate upside down to serve (crust will now be on the bottom and the meat on top). If desired, sprinkle grated cheese on top. Each pie serves 4 to 6 people.

Greenbrier—Porter's Creek Trail. "In the Spring, hike past the falls and it opens to a carpet of wildflowers."

—Sara Kane
Adoughable Things

Woodturner and Basket Shop

*I*n one of the distinctive trio of galleries in Turtle Hollow, Ross Markley turns local and imported woods into works of art. This award winning woodturner creates burl bowls, sculpture, and wall hangings from red oak, bleached maple, cherry, walnut, Australian eucalyptus, and sassafras. When not working with wood, he makes jewelry, and is now delving into contemporary stone sculpture using alabaster, limestone, and marble.

In addition to his serious works, Ross makes many practical pieces for the kitchen; wooden salad bowls and servers, rolling pins, spatulas, spoons, and spurtles. Most of you are probably wondering what exactly is a spurtle. In his recipe instructions, Ross uses a spurtle to stir the ingredients. It was the first time I had heard of such a utensil. When I asked what it was, he explained it is a long round wooden stirring stick (Scottish in origin, used for preparing porridge), and is one of the first items a woodturner learns to turn on a lathe. It is one of his favorite cooking tools, as are all wooden cooking utensils. He says they do not mar pots and pans, feel good in your hand, and are easy to clean. And, contrary to what some believe, bacteria do not thrive on wood.

Turn them with a wooden spurtle or a spoon, but do try his **Woodturner's Chili** and **Turtle Hollow Caesar Salad**.

Woodturner's Chili

Ross Markley
WOODTURNER & BASKET SHOP

Handed down from one woodturner to another, 50 years of practice makes this chili what it is today. Ross serves this with hot garlic bread and cold beer. His **Turtle Hollow Caesar Salad** makes a great starter for this meal.

Ross wants you to be careful when broiling the beef. He says, "Stop! Do not broil a second beyond medium."

4 pounds eye of round
3 cloves garlic, sliced
1 pound hot Italian sausage
non-stick cooking spray
6 Vidalia onions, chopped
3 cloves garlic, minced
4 cans tomatoes (12 ounces each)

1 can tomato sauce (15 ounces)
4 cans red kidney beans (15 ounces each)
4 tablespoons chili powder ("more if you are over 21")
1 tablespoon salt
½ tablespoon pepper

1. Broil eye of round with sliced garlic (use knife to make small slits in meat to hold garlic). Broil until just medium (150°), do not over cook. Remove and set aside. Broil Italian sausage until done.

2. Coat bottom of large soup pot with cooking spray. Saute onions and garlic until tender, about 5 minutes. Add tomatoes, tomato sauce, kidney beans, chili powder, salt, and pepper. Simmer for 2 hours, stirring every ½ hour with wooden spurtle or spoon.

3. Slice broiled eye of round and sausage into ½" cubes and add to chili. Stir with spurtle until well blended. Simmer an additional ½ hour.

4. Before serving, heat soup tureen with hot water. Pour out water and add Chili. Leftover chili freezes well.

Real Texas Chili

Gena Lewis
LEWIS FAMILY CRAFTS

This recipe won the 1986 Chili Cookoff in Texas. It was given to Gena by a friend, Jesse Johnson, in Sargent, Texas who was co-inventor. Jesse, my kids thank you for helping to create a fantastic chili without beans!

2 tablespoons peanut oil
4 cups onion, chopped
6 garlic cloves, minced
2 jalapenos, chopped
6 pounds boneless chuck roast, finely diced
2 teaspoons cumin seeds

3 tablespoons oregano
3 ounces chili powder
2 cans whole tomatoes (28 ounces each)
7 cups water
salt and pepper to taste, optional

1. In a large Dutch oven, heat peanut oil. Saute onions, garlic, and jalapenos until tender. Remove from pan and set aside.

2. Combine meat, cumin seeds, and oregano. Brown in Dutch oven (this should be done in batches). Add back the vegetable mixture and the chili powder. Mix well. Add tomatoes and water.

3. Bring to a boil. Reduce heat and simmer for 2 to 3 hours. Adjust seasoning to your taste. Makes 12 to 16 large servings.

Note: Gena cuts this recipe in half for her family and still has enough for 2 or 3 meals.

"We enjoy the Roaring Forks Motor Trail to see the streams (both rushing and lazy), the huge trees, and the original settlers cabins."

—Gena Lewis
Lewis Family Crafts

Bourboned Pork Roast

J. Alan Gribbins
THE J. ALAN GALLERY

The bourbon and brown sugar give this roast a slightly sweet taste. The pan drippings from this roast are so fantastic, you will be tempted to drink them. After adding and igniting the bourbon to the roast, you could sneak a few par-boiled potatoes in the pan to cook along with the roast.

3 to 5 pound pork loin roast	2 tablespoons flour
2 tablespoons spicy brown mustard	1 cup brown sugar
salt and pepper to taste	1 ½ tablespoons oil
2 garlic cloves, minced	½ cup bourbon

1. Rub roast with mustard, salt, pepper, and garlic. Mix together flour and brown sugar. Press mixture onto roast. Brown, on top of stove, in heated oil in roasting pan or a large black iron skillet.

2. Place browned roast in 450° oven for 15 to 20 minutes, until very brown. Remove pan from oven. Place on open oven door, or another safe place. Carefully pour bourbon over roast. Standing back with an outstretched arm, ignite with a long match (use caution—it will ignite immediately, shooting up blue flames a couple of feet into air). Let flames burn out naturally (takes about 1 minute).

3. Cover roast with foil. Return to oven and reduce heat to 350°. Roast for an additional 20 minutes per pound (1 hour for a 3 pound roast). Serve roast with gravy as is, or thicken with cornstarch.

Note: You may eliminate browning roast on top of oven first, and just brown it in the oven. It will not be as crisp on the outside, but is still delicious.

Variation: This recipe works equally well using a rolled veal chuck roast. Use the same method to cook and call it **Bourboned Veal Roast**. Try it with a Russian honey mustard.

Alice Moore Gallery

*H*iding behind the front row of shops in the Powdermill at Glades complex is Alice Moore's delightful garden and charming country house gallery. Both gallery and garden are so inviting you just cannot help but linger.

Many of Alice's watercolor art and calligraphy creations, are framed and matted with real pressed flowers. There are expressions of love and friendship, poems, scripture, and humorous scrolls. Alice will write messages on the back of the frame to personalize it for that "special someone." Wandering from room to room you will find her work displayed along with many fine gifts and crafts.

Alice definitely has a sense of humor. When I asked her for a recipe, she promised to give me one that feeds a crowd at cookouts. Upon opening the envelope, I realized this was one stew I would not be testing. After a good laugh together, Alice confessed that her usual contribution to a cookout is a can of beans and hot dogs on an open fire.

"Elephant Stew"

Alice Waugh Moore
ALICE MOORE GALLERY

Alice says "This will serve 3500 people or 190 hungry artists and craftsmen; if more are expected, 2 rabbits may be added, but only if necessary, because most folks don't like 'hare' in their stew."

1 elephant	400 cases canned browned gravy
salt and pepper	2 rabbits (optional)

1. Cut elephant into bite size pieces—this should take two months.

2. Add brown gravy to cover. Cook over wood fire for two weeks.

Quick "Stuffed" Pork Chops

Bobbie Adams
ADAMS MILL

I tested this recipe using one package of stuffing mix, but for those who really love stuffing, Bobbie says you may prepare it with two packages. For a special touch, saute some sliced mushrooms, chopped onions, and celery to mix into the stuffing before baking. Easy and quick to prepare, this recipe is great for family and company dinners.

4 to 6 pork chops	1 or 2 packages seasoned stuffing mix
salt and pepper	1 can cream of mushroom soup
onion powder	1 can water

1. Season pork chops to taste with salt, pepper, and onion powder. Brown in skillet. Transfer to 9" x 13" baking dish. Optional—saute mushrooms, onions, and celery in skillet for 5 minutes to be combined with stuffing.

2. Prepare stuffing according to package directions (add optional sauteed vegetables). Spread stuffing mix on top of pork chops. Mix together cream of mushroom soup and water. Pour over stuffing. Cover and bake at 350° for 45 to 60 minutes.

Pork Chops with Sherry

Kathy Shields Guttman

Since Carl Fogliani gave me a great story about pork chops, but no recipe, I decided to use one of my favorites. Next time you are in the mood for pork, stab your fork in a few of these chops.

6 pork chops, trim fat	fresh ground pepper
garlic powder	1 teaspoon olive oil
chili powder	½ cup sherry, plus ¼ cup
dried basil	1 teaspoon cornstarch
oregano	

1. Sprinkle chops with desired amounts of garlic powder, chili powder, basil, oregano, and pepper.

2. Heat oil in large skillet and brown chops on both sides. Add ½ cup sherry. Bring to a boil, then reduce to a simmer. Cover and cook for 30 minutes. Remove chops to a platter and keep warm.

3. Dissolve cornstarch in ¼ cup sherry. Stir in a tablespoon of the hot liquid from skillet into the cornstarch mixture. Add mixture to skillet, stirring constantly. Bring to a boil and then reduce heat to a simmer. Return chops to skillet and cook covered for an additional 5 minutes. Serve hot with rice or noodles.

Pork Chops for Sunday Dinner

Years ago, when I was dating a girl from a large family, I went to Sunday dinner at her house. There were 15 of us at the table. Her mother brought out a platter with 12 pork chops on it. As her father was giving the blessing, I looked up and saw everyone sitting there with their head bowed and a fork in their hand. When her father said 'Amen,' you wouldn't believe the fighting, stabbing, snarling, and over all bad manners that took over that family. But, I want you to know, that those were the best three pork chops I ever ate in my life…

—Carl Fogliani
Cosby Hillpeople Crafts

WHOP BISCUITS & FRIED APPLE PIE

Beans and Ham

Betty Jane Posey
BETTY JANE POSEY GALLERY

An old southern family recipe of Betty Jane's that may be prepared with navy beans, pinto beans, great northern beans, or black eyed peas. It is a southern tradition to eat black eyed peas on New Year's day. Some say if you have at least one bite of black eyed peas on New Year's, you will not go hungry the rest of the year. Others say having black eyed peas on New Year's will bring good luck and prosperity.

2 pounds dried beans
water to cover
1 ham hock (or country ham, bacon, or sugar cured ham)

3 medium onions, chopped
1 stalk celery, sliced thin
salt and pepper

1. In a large pot, precook dried beans by covering with water and bring to a full boil, then cover, remove from heat, and let sit one hour. Drain beans, rinse, then add fresh water to cover. Add ham hock, onions, celery, and salt and pepper to taste.

2. Bring to a medium boil, then cover and simmer until beans are soft, but not mushy, about 1 ½ to 2 hours. May be served immediately or reheated later.

"It is very important to me to continue in the intent and spirit of the founding members of the arts and crafts community, and offer a real working artist's studio which provides a learning experience as well. It is important, also, to offer for sale only that which I create."

—Betty Jane Posey
Betty Jane Posey Gallery

Pinto Beans & Dumplings

Annetta Hendrickson
THE LEATHER WORKS

Tired of chicken and dumplings? For a welcome change, try Annetta's Pinto Beans and Dumplings. The smoked ham hocks give this pot of beans an extra special flavor.

Beans

1 pound pinto beans, soaked overnight
2 smoked ham hocks

3 to 4 quarts water
salt and pepper

Dumplings

2 cups flour
¾ teaspoon salt
4 teaspoons baking powder

3 tablespoons butter
1 egg, beaten
¾ cup buttermilk

1. Soak beans overnight in enough water to cover beans. Discard water and rinse well. Place beans and smoked ham hocks in large soup pot. Add water. Bring to a boil and then reduce to a simmer. Cover and cook for 1 ½ to 2 hours until tender. Add salt and pepper. Remove ham hocks. Separate meat from bones and fat. Return meat to beans. Discard fat and bones.

2. Prepare dumplings and add to lightly boiling soup. Cook, without lifting lid (no peeking), for 25 minutes. The soup may be prepared early in the day, or the day before, and brought back to a boil before adding dumplings.

3. To prepare dumplings: Sift together flour, salt, and baking powder. Cut in butter until crumbly. Mix egg with milk. Pour slowly into flour, mixing with fork to form a stiff batter. Roll out on floured surface. Cut into 1" x 2" strips.

Barbecue Sauce with Chicken Wings

Buie Boling
BUIE POTTERY

Buie says this is a good all-around sauce, and is particularly good baked on chicken wings. This recipe was given to Buie by her mother, Jane Boling. Be sure to serve steamed rice, or French bread, with this dish to take advantage of the excellent sauce.

Barbecue Sauce

2 tablespoons oil
1 onion, chopped
6 tablespoons ketchup
1 teaspoon Worcestershire sauce
½ cup water
3 tablespoons vinegar

2 teaspoons sugar
¾ teaspoon dry mustard
¼ teaspoon salt
⅛ teaspoon pepper
1 teaspoon paprika

Chicken

3 to 4 pounds chicken wings

1. Heat oil in saucepan and saute onion for about 5 minutes until tender. Add ketchup, Worcestershire sauce, water, vinegar, sugar, dry mustard, salt, pepper, and paprika. Stir well and remove from heat.

2. Place wings in 9" x 13" pan. Pour barbecue sauce over wings. Bake at 350° for 50 minutes, basting every 15 minutes. Serves 6 to 8.

Variation: Place 10 pieces of skinned chicken breasts and thighs in 9" x 13" pan. Par boil some quartered potatoes for 10 minutes. Place in pan with chicken. Pour barbecue sauce over top. Bake at 350° for 1 ¼ hours, basting every 15 minutes.

"I don't go in the kitchen much, but I have a craft hint—have lots of patience or find another job!"

—Buie Boling

The Woodware Co.

*J*ean Yett Moore, originally from Sevierville, Tennessee, has followed more than one career path in her life. After studying art at the University of Mississippi, she got side-tracked for 14 ½ years as a police officer in Texas.

While in Texas, she and her husband, Darell, started doing craft shows. After several shows in the Gatlinburg area, they decided to move back home to the Smoky Mountains and open a studio. They make customized keepsake boxes, wooden Christmas ornaments, unique name items, educational puzzles, and much more.

Jean cherishes her Smoky Mountain roots and memories. Her grandparents ran Yett's Dairy. Her father delivered the first pasteurized milk in the Smokies. Her grandmother Mimmy put on "an unbelievable spread of food for all the family." Jean and her cousins would play in the pasture and barn until lunch (except for the time they were chased out of the pasture by an old cow that didn't like girls).

When Jean is not churning out wooden crafts in her studio, she enjoys creating new recipes. Her original recipe for **Fiesta Chicken** is proof of her creative capability in both studio and kitchen.

Fiesta Chicken

Jean Yett Moore
WOODWARE CO.

A creative concoction of chicken, green chili, and cheese, this original recipe by Jean is a winner. When testing the recipe, I used the pan juices to pour over the rice; and garnished the platter with fresh cilantro and thick slices of roasted red pepper.

8 skinless, boneless chicken breast pieces
garlic powder
onion powder
salt or salt substitute
pepper
1 pound mozzarella cheese
1 can whole green chilies, drained
4 cups cooked rice (plain or Spanish)

1. In a large foil-lined baking pan, arrange chicken pieces so they do not overlap each other. Lightly sprinkle each piece with garlic and onion powder. Salt and pepper to taste, or use a good salt substitute.

2. Slice mozzarella so you can place a generous slice of cheese on each piece of chicken. Slice chilies down one side and remove seeds. Place spread out chilies on top of cheese.

3. Cover and bake at 350° for 45 minutes or until chicken is done. Serve arranged on top of a bed of plain or Spanish rice on a large platter.

Use garlic powder instead of excessive salt. It lends a salty taste without the sodium.
—Jean Moore
The Woodware Co.

Chicken Parmesan

Eleanor Hopf
SHUCKS Y'ALL

This recipe is a snap to prepare and delicious to eat. While the chicken is baking, toss up a salad and prepare some garlic bread.

1 ½ pounds skinned and deboned
    chicken breasts
2 eggs, beaten
Italian bread crumbs

2 tablespoons olive oil
1 jar spaghetti sauce
1 cup grated mozzarella cheese

1. Dip chicken breasts in egg. Roll in Italian bread crumbs. Brown both sides in olive oil.

2. Place browned chicken in a 9" x 13" pan. Pour spaghetti sauce over chicken. Cover with foil. Bake at 350° for 20 to 30 minutes.

3. Remove from oven and sprinkle mozzarella cheese on top. Bake uncovered for another 10 minutes.

"I learned from my grandmother it is not polite to ask someone for their recipe. God forbid if you do that! You tell them how good it is, and that you would like to make it. If they give it to you, fine, but you don't ask."

—Eleanor Hopf
Shucks Y'All!

Chicken with Wine

Wilma Prebor
QUILTS BY WILMA

This recipe takes a little effort to prepare, but it is worth it. The aroma and flavor of this dish is a delight to the senses. If you do not have sherry, you may use Vermouth or a dry white wine.

¼ cup butter, or margarine
1 chicken, cut up (or 8 chicken pieces)
1 large onion, cut in rings
1 large clove garlic, minced
4 chicken bouillon cubes
2 cups hot water

¼ cup blending flour
1 ½ tablespoons cold water
8 ounces sliced fresh mushrooms (or canned)
salt and pepper to taste
½ cup sherry

1. In large skillet, melt butter. Brown chicken on one side. Remove from pan. Add onions and garlic to pan and stir. Dissolve bouillon cubes in water and add to pan.

2. In a small bowl, make a paste by mixing blending flour with water (if you use all-purpose flour, use only 3 tablespoons). Add paste slowly to broth, whisking until smooth. Return chicken to skillet. Add mushrooms, salt, and pepper. Cover and simmer for 1 ½ hours.

3. Remove cover and add sherry. Bring back to a boil and then serve. Serves 4 to 6.

"Buying a quilt should be a personal thing. Look at a quilt and you know 'that's the one,' if it just calls to you. It may not be the colors in your room, but it doesn't have to be."

—Wilma Prebor
Quilts By Wilma

Honey Mustard Chicken Breasts

Kathy Shields Guttman

Inspired by Sara Kane's recipe for **Honey Mustard Salad Dressing**, I created this dish. It is a nice change from coating raw chicken with beaten egg before rolling it in bread crumbs. Experiment with different bread crumbs, ground nuts, and herbs in your quest for different tastes.

1 pound boneless, skinless chicken
   breast strips
2 tablespoons Honey Mustard Salad
   Dressing
1 cup seasoned Italian bread crumbs
⅓ cup ground pecan meal

¼ teaspoon garlic powder
½ teaspoon salt
½ teaspoon dried basil
¼ teaspoon oregano
2 tablespoons olive oil

1. Coat chicken with Honey Mustard Salad Dressing. Mix together bread crumbs, pecan meal, garlic powder, salt, basil, and oregano. Dip coated chicken into crumb mixture. Let rest for 10 minutes before cooking.

2. In a large skillet, heat olive oil. When hot, add chicken strips. Cook for 4 to 5 minutes on each side until golden brown. Serves 4.

To warm pewter plates before serving a meal, run hot water on each plate for a few seconds and then dry. This is done to put heat into the plate so that heat in the food will stay in the food. Never put pewter on stove or in oven to warm. It has a very low melting point.

—John Thomas
Pewter by Hedko

Lime Marinated Chicken

Kathy Shields Guttman

"Mmmm delicious" is the best way to describe this chicken's tart, tangy taste. For a little extra pizzazz, baste with a little honey garlic barbecue sauce for the last 5 minutes of cooking. You may cook and freeze the chicken, or freeze the uncooked chicken pieces in the marinade, then defrost and cook.

10 to 12 skinned thighs & breasts	1 teaspoon paprika
¼ cup vegetable oil	½ teaspoon chili powder
½ cup fresh lime juice	½ teaspoon thyme
2 teaspoons salt	½ teaspoon garlic powder
2 teaspoons onion powder	barbecue sauce, optional
2 teaspoons basil	

1. Place chicken pieces in large ziplock plastic bag. In a mixing bowl, combine oil, lime juice, salt, onion powder, basil, paprika, chili powder, thyme, and garlic powder. Stir well and pour over chicken pieces. Seal bag and place in refrigerator overnight (or for at least 4 hours).

2. Remove chicken from refrigerator to bring to room temperature before grilling (about 30 minutes). Pre-heat barbecue and grill chicken pieces until done (about 12 to 15 minutes per side). Baste often with marinade and, if desired, baste with barbecue sauce for the last 5 minutes of cooking.

Variation: You may use boneless skinned chicken breasts for this recipe. Reduce cooking time accordingly.

Artist Dolls by Myriam/Cobblestones

I really wanted to highlight Myriam Nolcken in this book in order to tell you about her unique cobblestone creations and artists dolls. This talented artisan, originally from Estonia, transforms simple river stones into incredibly detailed animals and theme dolls.

Through personal experimentation, she developed a technique she calls Cobblestone Sculpture. She paints and sculpts smooth river stones to create a wide diversity of animals.

Her artist dolls are an outgrowth of the cobblestone sculpture. Each anatomical feature is a separate selected stone or pebble used to articulate even such tiny details as its fingers and hands. The faces are handpainted and then the hair and garments are made to fit the theme of the doll. The theme of each original doll reflects the regions of the four separate continents on which she has lived and worked.

Myriam and Ron Nolcken do not devote much time to cooking and planning meals. They were somewhat hesitant to participate in this cookbook. But after a little persistent nudging, Ron agreed to tell me about his method of catching and cooking free-range fowl.

Sauteed Free Range Fowl

Ron Nolcken
Artist Dolls by Myriam/Cobblestones

Ron and Myriam Nolcken raise their own chickens, ducks, geese, and guinea fowl. The fowl run loose on their fenced property in the hollows of East Tennessee. When not out hunting for cobblestones for Myriam's lovely creations, Ron may be out hunting their fowl for dinner. He says "Range fowl are not the soft meat which you get at the supermarket, they are more like wild game. Roasting the whole bird produces tough meat, so we skin the chicken, remove the meat and saute and simmer it."

Not having access to free range fowl, I have not tested this recipe, but have given you Ron's method of preparing it. He assures me it produces tender, delicious results. He serves it with steamed rice, or noodles, and green beans.

 1 free range fowl, skin removed   **1 to 2 tablespoons vegetable oil**

1. Heat oil in black iron skillet. Brown meat on medium heat. Cover and reduce heat to low. Allow meat to simmer and steam for about 1 hour, or until tender.

"An axiom of life is that most of the smoothest rocks are always going to be on the far side of the stream. That's my version of the 'grass is always greener.'"

—Ron Nolcken
Cobblestone Creations

Sesame Chicken

Kathy Shields Guttman

I created this dish about 15 years ago. I make it with the soup mix, soy sauce, and sesame oil for a quick family meal. For company I dress it up with mushroom caps, onions, and pepper slices. Be sure and serve it with steamed rice to take full advantage of the sauce.

8 to 10 chicken pieces
garlic powder, optional
1 package dry onion soup
3 tablespoons soy sauce
1 tablespoon flavored sesame seed oil

1 sliced onion, optional
8 to 10 mushrooms, optional
green and/or red pepper slices,
   optional

1. Place chicken pieces in 11" x 14" roasting pan. Sprinkle with garlic powder, onion soup, soy sauce, and sesame seed oil. Cover with aluminum foil and bake for 50 minutes at 350°.

2. Uncover and baste with sauce. Add any or all of the vegetables and baste again. Bake uncovered for another 25 minutes, basting every 10 minutes. Serves 4 to 6.

Sue's Fried Chicken

Sue Ownby
E & T Woodcarvings

This fried chicken beats the Colonel's any day. By removing the chicken skin, you don't feel guilty about eating it fried. The flour mixture gives it a crisp texture on the outside and allows the meat to stay moist on the inside. This recipe is equally good served hot or cold. No wonder it is one of Sue's favorite picnic meals.

6 to 8 chicken pieces	½ teaspoon salt
1 egg, beaten	¼ teaspoon pepper
½ cup flour	vegetable oil for frying

1. Remove skin from chicken. Coat each piece with egg. Place flour, salt, and pepper into a paper or plastic bag. Drop chicken pieces, one at a time, into flour mixture and shake well to coat.

2. Heat oil in frying pan (Sue uses a black iron skillet). When oil is hot, carefully drop in chicken pieces. Fry until chicken is a light golden brown, then cover pan and reduce heat to simmer for approximately 25 to 35 minutes. Drain on paper towel before serving.

Variation: If you do not like to fry chicken in oil, place flour coated chicken pieces on a wire cookie rack and place on foil-lined baking sheet. Bake in oven at 375° for approximately 45 to 55 minutes.

When you splatter grease on clothes, put flour or powder on stain.

—Sue Ownby
E & T Woodcarvings

Chicken Casserole

Clarice Maples
HEMLOCK FALLS RENTALS

This recipe is guaranteed to please even the pickiest of eaters. When tested by my family and friends, it was given a unanimous thumbs up.

Instead of using only breast meat, you may use the meat from a whole chicken. It is a great way to use the boiled chicken meat when making chicken soup.

1 box butter-flavored snack crackers	8 ounces sliced mushrooms, fresh or
¾ cup margarine, melted	canned
4 chicken breasts, stewed, skinned,	2 cups sour cream
and boned	2 cans cream of chicken soup

1. In a large bag, crush crackers into crumbs. Mix margarine with cracker crumbs. Place a thin layer of mixture on bottom of a 9" x 13" baking dish, reserving the rest for top layer. Add a layer of chicken pieces and sliced mushrooms.

2. Mix the sour cream and cream of chicken soup together. Pour over the chicken mixture. Place remaining crumbs on top. Bake at 350° for 15 to 20 minutes or until hot. Serves 4 to 6.

Note: Sometimes Clarice uses 1 can cream of chicken soup and 1 can cream of mushroom. I tried it using cream of celery soup. Experiment with different soups.

Make your own spackling compound. Just make a paste of baking soda and Elmer's Glue and rub it into place.

—Clarice Maples
Hemlock Falls Nightly Rentals

Chicken Stuffing Casserole

Garnet Weiss
<small>Woods by Weiss</small>

This recipe Garnet received from her friend, Kay Greene, makes a delicious entree for family or company meals. You can have fun trying different combinations of soups, stuffings, and chicken pieces with this recipe. Try it with broccoli cheddar soup, bread stuffing, and chicken thighs; or golden mushroom soup, cornbread stuffing, and cooked turkey meat.

6 pieces chicken breast
1 can cream of celery soup
1 can cream of chicken soup

1 can water
1 package cornbread stuffing
½ cup melted butter

1. Lay chicken pieces in 9" x 13" pan. Mix soups and water together. Pour over chicken.

2. Sprinkle dry stuffing over mixture. Pour melted butter over stuffing. Bake at 350° for 45 minutes. Serves 4 to 6.

"Creating is very fulfilling. There is a special part of yourself that goes into each piece. Being a member of GSACC is an opportunity to work together to promote our crafts and share ideas."

—Garnet Weiss
Woods by Weiss

Cornish Hens and Rice

Annetta Hendrickson
THE LEATHER WORKS

Cornish hens may be considered elegant fare, carefully removing the delicate meat with a fork, alongside glowing candles and a glass of wine. Or, for a casual presentation, lay out the checkered tablecloth, lots of napkins, and devour the meat using your hands. Served casual, or formal, this recipe handed down to Annetta from her mother, is simply delicious.

1 box chicken flavored rice & vermi-
celli mix
2 Cornish game hens, split in half
½ cup butter or margarine
4 tablespoons apple jelly

1 teaspoon thyme
1 teaspoon dried crushed mint
2 tablespoons soy sauce
salt and pepper to taste

1. Prepare rice according to package directions, but boil for only 3 minutes. Pour into a large lightly greased baking dish. Place hens on top of rice.

2. In a small saucepan, melt margarine. Add jelly, thyme, mint, soy sauce, salt, and pepper. Stir well. Brush mixture liberally over hens. Cover and bake at 375° for 50 to 60 minutes until hens are tender. Serves 4.

"My favorite places in the Smokies? Anywhere in the mountains I can be alone and absorb the peace and tranquility these mountains give so freely."

—Annetta Hendrickson
Leather Works

Smoked Turkey Deli Sandwich

Joan McGill
GLADES DELI

This hearty sandwich will satisfy the most ravenous of appetites. I like to leave out the mayo and include a slice or two of fresh avocado. Make up a few of these sandwiches, grab a bag of chips and some pop, and have a picnic!

¼ pound sliced smoked turkey	lettuce
2 slices smoked cheddar cheese	tomato
6" hoagie roll	mayonnaise

1. Place turkey and cheese on inside of roll. Put in microwave for about 30 seconds until cheese is melted. Serve plain or with your choice of lettuce, tomato, and mayonnaise.

$500 Free Duck Dinner

Mac convinced me to have a big duck dinner for family and friends by telling me "It's going to be free. It isn't going to cost us anything."

So he and three other hunters headed off to a pond that had wild ducks. One hunter was supposed to fire a shot to get the ducks to fly. The others were then going to shoot the ducks. Well the ducks got airborne alright, but as Mac pulled the trigger on his double barrel gun, it went click, click. The safety was stuck. He gave it a quick touch. It went off with both barrels pushing the gun right back and slicing his finger to the bone. A trip to the hospital, a nice stitch job, and a $500 bill later, we all had Mac's "free" duck dinner.

—Susan McDonell
Gemstone

Batter Fried Fish

Carl Fogliani
Cosby Hillpeople Crafts

This is more of a method than a recipe, for frying fish or seafood. Make up a batch of these dry ingredients and keep on hand for coating your fish. This may be used for pan frying, broiling, or deep frying fish. Carl's favorite fish to fry is flounder, but he also fries up batches of sole, shrimp, and scallops. His recipe for **Hushpuppies** makes the perfect side dish for a good old-fashioned fish fry.

Dry ingredients

> 2 cups cornmeal
> 1 cup flour
> ½ teaspoon salt

> ¼ teaspoon black pepper
> ¼ teaspoon garlic powder

Marinade

> **milk or egg**

1. Combine cornmeal, flour, salt, pepper, and garlic powder and store in an air-tight container.

2. Marinate fish or seafood in milk (or egg, for a richer batter) for 15 minutes. Place dry ingredients (use about 1 cup for each pound of fish) on a plate. Roll fish in dry ingredients until well coated. Allow to sit for at least 5 minutes before frying.

3. Broil, pan fry, or deep-fry until golden brown. Do not over-cook.

"The winter months are spent getting ready for the season; but, any more, it seems that the busy season never ends. We get more and more tourists during the winter. Personally, I think it is the best time to visit Gatlinburg."
—Carl Fogliani
Cosby Hillpeople Crafts

Chef Jock's Fish Fillets

Giacomo "Jock" Lijoi
Tastebuds Cafe

The best seats in the house at Tastebuds Cafe are out on the front porch. This wonderful restaurant in Wears Valley has an incredible view of the Smoky Mountains. Just as memorable as the view, is Chef Jock's talent in the kitchen. If you are visiting the area, do make a point to dine at his restaurant.

4 six ounce fillets (mahi mahi, roughy, or grouper)	1 tablespoon chopped shallots
½ cup water	1 teaspoon chopped parsley
½ cup dry white wine	¼ teaspoon chopped garlic
¼ cup butter or margarine	1 ½ tablespoons chopped tomatoes
	¼ to ½ cup heavy cream

1. Place fish fillets in 9" x 13" glass baking dish. Add enough water and wine to fill pan half way up the fillets. Do not cover fish completely with liquid. Bake at 400° for 20 to 30 minutes or until white juice begins to rise from fillets. If desired, you may saute fish in liquid in large skillet until tender, about 10 to 15 minutes. Remove fish from oven or stove.

2. In a medium skillet, melt butter. Saute shallots, parsley, garlic, and tomatoes on high heat, stirring frequently. Do not brown or burn. Add ½ cup of liquid from cooked fish. Heat on high and reduce liquid by ⅓ (takes about 3 to 5 minutes), stirring frequently. Add ¼ to ½ cup heavy cream and reduce liquid by ⅓ to ½, depending on how thick and rich you like sauce.

3. Place fillets on serving plate and pour sauce on top. Good served with rice and sauteed vegetables.

Quilted Rose Seafood Casserole

Maria Holloway
HOLLOWAY'S COUNTRY HOME

This recipe is an original creation by Maria. You may use fresh, frozen, or canned crab meat. The ingredients may be kept on hand in pantry and freezer. A quick easy dinner for unexpected guests, serve with steamed rice to take advantage of its delicious juices.

½ pound crab meat
½ pound scallops (or peeled shrimp)
½ cup shredded Monterey Jack cheese
1 small can french fried onion rings (halved)

1 can cream of shrimp soup (or cream of mushroom soup)
½ cup milk
2 cups frozen vegetables (cauliflower & broccoli)
½ cup sliced mushrooms, optional

1. Preheat oven to 350°. Grease a large round casserole dish. In a mixing bowl, combine all ingredients together saving half the can of fried onion rings.

2. Pour mixture into casserole dish. Bake for 1 hour covered, then remove cover. Top with remaining fried onion rings. Lower oven to 300° and continue to bake for 15 minutes. Allow to set uncovered 10 minutes before serving. Good served with rice. Makes 4 to 6 servings.

Recipe for a Happy Life

Maria Holloway
HOLLOWAYS COUNTRY HOME

Love
Patience
Hard work

Joy
A love of Art

1. Piece together like a fine patchwork quilt. Carefully choose the pieces for which to use. Stitch together with love, patience, hard work, and joy.

2. The results will be rewarded with generation after generation of warm lasting memories.

Salmon Patties for the '90s

Kathy Shields Guttman

This is a spiced up version of an old family favorite. These patties freeze well and may be reheated in oven or microwave.

8 ounce can sockeye salmon
2 green onions, chopped
¼ cup grated zucchini
¼ cup grated carrot
1 tablespoon salsa

fresh chopped cilantro or parsley
½ cup bread crumbs
1 egg
1 tablespoon oil for frying
cornmeal, optional

1. In a medium mixing bowl, combine salmon, green onions, zucchini, carrots, salsa, cilantro, bread crumbs, and egg. Mix thoroughly and form into individual patties.

2. Heat oil on medium high heat in large skillet. Place patties (as is, or coated in cornmeal) in heated oil. Fry until browned on each side (about 4 minutes per side). Serve as is, or with salsa on top. Makes 5 or 6 patties.

Joan's Tuna Salad

Joan McGill
GLADES DELI

The chopped egg whites lighten the texture and taste of this tuna salad. Joan suggests trying it on a hoagie bun, or your favorite bread, along with lettuce, tomato, and mayonnaise, for a wholesome good sandwich.

6 ounce can light tuna, drained
2 hard boiled eggs, whites only, finely
  chopped

¼ cup green olives, chopped
¼ cup pickles, chopped
½ cup mayonnaise

1. Flake tuna. Add egg whites, olives, pickles, and mayonnaise. Blend well. Eat as is, or make into a sandwich. Serves 2 to 3.

Yacht Club Tuna

John Thomas
PEWTER BY HEDKO

While testing this recipe, I had a kitchen full of people and I was trying to hurry. Not paying strict attention to John's instructions, I read apples in the ingredients list and proceeded to chop them up and add them to the tuna. I learned two things that day: 1) Always read the ingredients and instructions carefully before proceeding with the recipe; and 2) Not all mistakes are bad. The chopped apple gave it a crunchy texture and taste such as you might find in a Waldorf Salad.

6 ½ ounce can solid white albacore tuna, drained	3 medium sweet gherkins, chopped
½ cup mayonnaise	⅛ cup pecans, chopped
2 celery stalks, chopped	1 medium red delicious apple, sliced
	crackers

1. In a medium bowl thoroughly mix tuna, mayonnaise, celery, pickles, and pecans. Allow tuna to remain in chunks (John says "We are not making a spread here!"). Cover and refrigerate.

2. Just before serving, slice apple into ¼" sections. Arrange on two plates in semi-circle (½ apple per plate). Place tuna salad on inside arc of apples and serve with your favorite crackers on the side. Serves 2.

Family Reunion

For my grandmother's 90th birthday, we had a big family reunion. We had barbecue of all descriptions for lunch, allowing for different tastes and health considerations and a birthday cake with 90 candles in different colors. Since relatives came from all over, and because some cousins, etc. had never met, we had T-shirts printed for the occasion. One side of the family wore blue, another wore yellow. So, of course, the combining of those families (and colors) were in green. Special friends were in red. In a mere glance, everyone knew something about each other before they even met.

—John Thomas
Pewter By Hedko

VEGETABLES & SIDE DISHES

Broccoli Casserole

Margaret Seymour
Seymour's Country Crafts

Tired of meat and potatoes? Try this delicious dairy casserole. My younger daughter usually disdains broccoli and rice. However, when mixed with processed cheese and cream of mushroom soup, even she had seconds.

1 cup minute rice, cooked	8 ounce jar processed cheese spread
10 ounces chopped broccoli, cooked	1 can cream of mushroom soup

1. Cook rice according to package directions. Add cooked broccoli to rice. Stir in cheese and cream of mushroom soup.

2. Preheat oven to 350°. Lightly grease a 2 quart round casserole. Pour in broccoli mixture. Bake for 30 to 35 minutes until hot and bubbly. Serves 4.

"My favorite hikes: Gunter Fork Cascades—at 8.2 miles in you do not ever meet any one. Spruce Flat Falls, beyond Greenbrier—one mile in and the beauty is not of this world. Mingo Falls—1/2 mile round trip—the very best of the close ones."

—Dick Seymour
Seymour's Country Crafts

Fried Cabbage

Betty Jane Posey
BETTY JANE POSEY GALLERY

On our first trip down to Tennessee, my husband and I became addicted to southern style cooked cabbage. Betty Jane's recipe is an excellent example of the way southerners prepare fried cabbage. To make it a vegetarian dish, you may delete the bacon and fry the cabbage with vegetable oil.

4 strips bacon	1 teaspoon sugar
1 medium head cabbage, shredded	salt and pepper
¾ to 1 cup water	

1. Place bacon in cold black iron skillet. Cook slowly over medium low heat, turning often, until browned. Remove bacon and drain on paper towel. Crumble into pieces.

2. Add cabbage, all at once, to bacon drippings. Add water, sugar, salt, pepper, and bacon. Stir well. Cover and simmer until tender, about 20 to 30 minutes.

3. Remove cover from pan. Turn heat to medium high. Cook rapidly, stirring frequently, until all liquid is absorbed. Serve immediately, or reheat later in microwave.

"Cooking became our main thing that winter. We became quite good at it. My fried cabbage became legendary."

—Betty Jane Posey
Betty Jane Posey Gallery

Village Candles

*R*ichard Lang has been making candles for over 70 years. At the age of 13 he started it as a hobby. After 30 years in banking and investing, a connection in the space industry enabled him to retire from the financial world to a full time career in candlemaking. His connection taught him to make candle molds out of silicone. These molds revolutionized the candle business and changed his life.

Richard and Stephanie Lang's studio make more than 900 different candles. From the original little mouse with big ears to a nine piece set of Scrooge and The Spirit of Christmas, to handpainted American Eagles, Humming Birds and Roosters, and tiny little farm animals that are perfect on a birthday cupcake, there is a candle to please everyone.

Richard Lang is a man of many talents and abilities, not the least of which is his kitchen wizardry. In his younger years he says he cooked with "reckless abandon." With his collection of over 290 cookbooks, he likes to combine ideas from five or six cookbooks to come up with his own version of a recipe. Loving German food, he has developed some tasty recipes for **Baked Sauerkraut** and **Red Cabbage**.

Baked Sauerkraut

Richard Lang
VILLAGE CANDLES

Mr. Lang loves German cooking. He received this recipe for Baked Sauerkraut from his mother. The brown sugar gives it an interesting sweet twist from the more traditional sauerkraut recipes.

8 ounces Kielbossa smoked sausage	1 teaspoon caraway seeds
1 apple, peeled and sliced	2 tablespoons brown sugar
1 can sauerkraut, drained	water

1. Preheat oven to 350°. Line bottom of 2 quart round baking dish with thinly sliced Kielbossa sausage. Place the sliced apples over sausage.

2. Combine sauerkraut and caraway seeds and place over sausage and apples. Sprinkle brown sugar on top. Fill baking dish with water (about 1 to 1 ½ cups) to just cover sauerkraut. Bake for about 1 ½ hours.

"A Rose of a Different Color"

When I first brought my wife, Stephanie, into the studio to teach her how to make candles, I showed her how to make a rose bud on a pillar. I showed her how to shade the petals by painting a pink one and then a yellow one. "Now you try it," I told her, "you don't have to do it like I do." When I turned around and saw her making a blue rose, I thought "Oh brother—a blue rose! Well, when she's not here during the week, I'll put it on the half price table and it won't be a dead loss."

When she finished with it, I put it with a half dozen others I had made earlier. About 10 minutes later three women came through the door. One of them made a bee line straight for that blue rose! She said "That is just what I've been looking for. Everything in my living room is blue, and that's exactly what I wanted!" Now we sell purple cows, pink geese, and a lot of colorful roses.

—Richard Lang
Village Candles

Red Cabbage

Richard Lang
VILLAGE CANDLES

Richard Lang developed this recipe using the "trial & error" method. A colorful and slightly sweet side dish, this would go great with breaded veal cutlets and Lorraine Quilliam's **Zucchini Rounds.** For dessert try serving Wilma's **Lemon Dream Bars.**

2 strips bacon, cut in small pieces	½ cup raisins
1 teaspoon butter	½ cup red wine
1 small head red cabbage, shredded	2 tablespoons grape jelly
1 small apple, peeled, cored, and sliced	¼ teaspoon salt

1. Fry bacon in a skillet until crisp. Drain well on paper towel.

2. In a 2 quart saucepan, melt butter. Stir in bacon pieces, cabbage, apple, raisins, red wine, grape jelly, and salt. Cover and simmer until cabbage is tender; takes about 15 minutes.

Foil Roasted Corn on the Cob

Charlotte Boles
Whispering Pines Woodcrafts

This works great for cookouts, barbecues, and picnics. The ice keeps the corn fresh and cool when taking it to a cookout at your favorite campground. And the best thing is there are no pots to clean!

heavy duty aluminum foil	6 to 8 ears of corn
margarine	8 ice cubes

1. Tear off a large sheet of aluminum foil, about 18" x 30". Lightly grease foil with margarine. Remove husks and silks from corn. Place corn in center of foil. Add ice cubes. Fold foil together to tightly seal all edges.

2. Place wrapped corn on heated campfire grill or barbecue. Roast for about 20 minutes. The ice cubes melt and steam the corn. Delicious!

Leather Britches Beans

In times not too long ago here in the mountains, there was no electricity for refrigeration. Food preservation had to be innovative. The chief method of preserving food for the winter was canning, but sometimes a family could not afford enough canning jars and lids. The drying of fruit to preserve it was already known, so the people adapted this technique to the drying of green beans and pole beans.

Try this method yourself for Leather Britches Beans. As soon as beans are harvested, string them up for about a month to dry. They will shrivel and brown. To use, rehydrate them by putting in pan with plenty of water to cover. Bring to a boil, remove from heat and let sit for one hour. Drain, rinse, and then add fresh water to cook. If you prefer, just let beans soak overnight in cold water, then drain and use.

—Betty Jane Posey
Betty Jane Posey Gallery

The J. Alan Gallery

A self-taught outsider artist, Alan Gribbins describes his work as contemporary and shys away from the word abstract. He primarily uses discs and lines to show feelings and expressions. Alan says "The most difficult work is the simplest. To make you feel with a few well placed lines and colors is an achievement. You're not going to see a house, you're not going to see rainfall, but it is my job to make you feel that."

Having painted in Cincinnati, Ohio "forever," Alan often visited Gatlinburg and loved the mountains. He was not sure his contemporary work would go over in Gatlinburg, but artist friends assured him that, with visitors from around the globe, his art would be accepted. He has lived in Gatlinburg for over two years now and people from large metropolitan cities and small little towns in Tennessee buy his work.

Alan's art may be contemporary, but some of his cooking is good old-fashioned country. His recipe for **Gribbins Green Beans** would fit right in with any down-home cooked meals.

Gribbins Green Beans

J. Alan Gribbins

J. Alan Gallery

Alan guarantees if you like good old country food, you will like these beans. His instructions for cooking them are "throw everything in a pot and cook them to death."

3 pounds green beans	hog jowl or pork hock
1 large onion, chopped	salt and pepper
½ green pepper, chopped	water
3 to 4 sprigs fresh dill	

1. Clean and snap green beans and place in a large soup pot of water. Add onions, green pepper, dill, hog jowl, and salt and pepper. Cover completely with water.

2. Bring to a quick boil and then turn down to a slow simmer for several hours until water cooks down. Stir every once in a while. Check to make sure water has not boiled out. The "cooked to death" process takes about 4 hours.

"One of my favorite places is the Little Pigeon River. Once, while having a quiet evening of reading and picnicing on a large flat rock in the middle of the river (at a spot where you look up for what seems like miles of rushing water lined on both sides by deep woods), I looked up to enjoy the view. My heart leapt … could it be … no, couldn't be—I went back to my reading. Drawn by the beauty of what I saw, I looked again and what I had assumed to be a configuration of beached limbs hanging on a boulder up river, began to move. Suddenly the largest white crane I had ever seen gracefully unfolded its wings and loped on over the water all the way up the river until it was out of sight."

—J. Alan Gribbins
J. Alan Gallery

Chili Roasted New Potatoes

Kathy Shields Guttman

These potatoes make a great side dish with poultry, fish, or eggs. I use a combination of red and white new potatoes. They come out crispy on the outside and tender inside.

2 pounds red and/or white new potatoes (about 6 medium)	1 teaspoon salt
	1 teaspoon chili powder
2 tablespoons olive oil	½ teaspoon dried basil
2 tablespoons fresh lemon juice	freshly ground pepper

1. Wash, dry, and dice new potatoes. Do not peel potatoes. In a large bowl, mix together olive oil, lemon juice, salt, chili powder, basil, and ground pepper. Add diced potatoes and mix to coat well.

2. Preheat oven to 400°. Place potatoes, with marinade, in lightly greased 9" x 13" pan. Roast, stirring every 15 minutes, for 45 to 55 minutes until brown.

Note: You may dice potatoes and let them sit in the marinade for 30 minutes before roasting—this gives it a more intense flavor.

"Being an artist is a mixed blessing. One day you thank God, the next you say 'Why me!'"

—J. Alan Gribbins
J. Alan Gallery

Curried Potatoes—Alu Sabje

Mary Louise Hunt
FIBER CREATIONS

Mary Louise has made three trips to India and has taught Indian cooking classes. She serves this authentic curried recipe with puris, an unleavened bread. I was mesmerized by the colors while preparing this dish. When adding the spices to the potatoes, the oil takes on an iridescent lime green color and the potatoes turn an intense golden yellow.

¼ cup vegetable oil
½ teaspoon mustard seeds
2 large potatoes, cubed
½ teaspoon fennel seeds
¼ teaspoon cayenne

¼ teaspoon cumin
1 teaspoon turmeric
½ teaspoon salt
1 bell pepper, chopped

1. Heat oil in a skillet and add mustard seeds. When they dance, (keep a wire mesh cover handy to prevent oil and seeds popping out and keeping seeds in pan) add potatoes.

2. Combine fennel seeds, cayenne, cumin, turmeric, and salt. Add all at once to potatoes. Stir well. Add bell pepper. Cover tightly and simmer until the potatoes are tender, about 15 minutes. Serves 2 to 4.

Adoughable Things by Nancy

*T*he largest Mixmaster I have ever seen hums away behind the counter as Nancy Hopf prepares the dough for her craft. There is no expiration date on her "Adoughable" items. These permanent pieces, however, look real enough to eat.

Nancy and Wes Hopf have been making and selling their dough products to delighted tourists for many years. Their product line includes individual fruit pie slices such as apple, blueberry, and cherry, as well as whole pies with a big slice cut out to show the plump and juicy fruit. In addition to pies, there are 3-D people, rolls, loaves, and lovely bread dough baskets ready to be filled with your own fresh biscuits and rolls. Because they will personalize items and do special orders, it is a great place to look for gifts to take back home.

After a busy day making dough products at the studio, Nancy confesses to using commercial pie shells to get dinner ready in a hurry. Her recipe for **Hamburger Pie** is quick, easy, and delicious. Although it takes a little more time to produce, do try her **Aunt Fanny's Baked Squash**, it is an excellent tasty dish.

Aunt Fanny's Baked Squash

Nancy Hopf
ADOUGHABLE THINGS BY NANCY

Nancy's adaptation of Aunt Fanny's Cabin (a restaurant in Smyrna, Georgia) Baked Squash is a crowd pleaser. Serve for company dinner or weekday meals. Squash sometimes has a bitter taste. The addition of the sugar in this recipe balances out the bitterness without making it sweet.

3 pounds yellow summer squash
½ cup chopped onion
2 tablespoons, plus ½ cup, cracker meal or breadcrumbs
2 eggs beaten, or 4 egg whites

½ cup butter, divided
1 tablespoon sugar
1 teaspoon salt, optional
½ teaspoon black pepper

1. Lightly grease (or use non-stick cooking spray) a 9" x 13" baking dish.

2. Clean and cut up squash. Boil with onion until tender, about 15 to 20 minutes. Drain thoroughly and mash. Add 2 tablespoons cracker meal, eggs, ¼ cup butter, sugar, salt, and pepper to squash. Mix well. Pour mixture into baking dish.

3. Spread ½ cup cracker meal on top. Melt ¼ cup butter and pour on top of cracker meal. Bake at 375° for about 1 hour or until brown on top. Serves 8 to 10.

Note: You may cut the recipe in half and bake in an 8" square dish.

Summer Squash Delight

Victoria Azpurua
Homespun Heart

Different cooks interpret recipes in different ways. I tested this recipe using zucchini squash sliced in ¼" rounds. When cooked, it maintained it's shape and combined nicely with the onion for a chunky style dish.

I sent my friend Peggy this recipe to prepare and bring to a taste-testing dinner party. She used pepper squash (similar to an acorn squash). The texture was smooth and creamy, like mashed potatoes.

I called Victoria to ask what she uses in this recipe. Yellow crookneck was her answer. All three versions are delightfully delicious.

1 cup margarine	3 large onions, chunked
8 to 10 summer squash (sliced in pieces)	2 to 3 garlic cloves, minced
	garlic salt

1. In a large pan, melt margarine and add squash and onions. Add garlic cloves and garlic salt to taste.

2. Cook covered over medium heat until tender, about 15 to 20 minutes. Serves 8 to 12.

Note: You may reduce margarine to ½ cup, or even ¼ cup. It will be less rich, but still delicious.

Fried Green Tomatoes

Betty Jane Posey
Betty Jane Posey Gallery

Since testing Betty Jane's recipe, I've become addicted to this southern specialty. I've dipped them in: white cornmeal, yellow cornmeal, plain breadcrumbs, and Italian breadcrumbs; melted cheddar cheese, jack cheese, and goat cheese on top; served them with salsa and red pepper jelly. I've spread them with olive oil instead of dipping them in egg. Experiment with your own variations and enjoy!

green tomatoes, in ¼" to ½" slices	salt and pepper
1 egg, beaten	vegetable or bacon drippings
cornmeal	

1. Dip tomato slices in beaten egg. Coat slices with mixture of cornmeal, salt, and pepper.

2. Heat oil in large skillet. Fry tomatoes until brown and tender. Serve hot.

"Steaks Cheap for Lunch, Come on Down"

One evening, when we owned the Owl's Nest Restaurant, the freezer was accidently left open. The next day all the steaks and meat had thawed. Rather than throwing out $500 worth of meat, we sent word all over town we would be "serving steaks cheap for lunch, so come on down." All up and down the Parkway people were saying "You better go down there fast, they're cooking steaks today for two dollars and a half." Everybody in town showed up. We didn't lose the freezer full of food. We cooked it, we served it, and they ate it, all in one day!

—Betty Jane Posey
Betty Jane Posey Gallery

Zucchini Rounds

Lorraine Quilliam
BUCKHORN HANDCRAFTS

These fried vegetable pancakes are crisp and lightly browned on the outside and moist and tender inside. Try adding a ½ teaspoon of dried basil and a dash of oregano to the batter for an extra added Italian taste.

⅓ cup packaged biscuit mix	2 eggs, gently beaten
¼ cup grated Parmesan cheese	2 cups shredded zucchini
⅛ teaspoon pepper	2 tablespoons margarine

1. In a mixing bowl, stir together biscuit mix, cheese, and pepper. Stir in eggs just until moistened. Fold in zucchini.

2. Melt margarine in a large skillet over medium heat. Drop 2 tablespoons of batter into margarine for each round. Cook for about 2 to 3 minutes on each side, or until brown. Makes 8 rounds.

CHEESE & EGGS

Eggs Goldenrod

Betty Jane Posey
BETTY JANE POSEY GALLERY

This is one of Betty Jane's favorite ways to serve eggs. Treat your family to this delicious recipe for Sunday breakfast or brunch, or as a luncheon dish or light supper.

Eggs Goldenrod

4 hard-boiled eggs
white sauce
8 slices buttered toast

8 slices crisp bacon (or simulated bacon bits)

White Sauce

2 tablespoons butter
2 tablespoons flour
¼ teaspoon salt

dash pepper
1 cup milk

1. While eggs are boiling, make white sauce. Cool and dice eggs. Make toast and fry bacon.

2. Place toast on plate. Cover with warm white sauce. Sprinkle eggs on sauce. Crumble bacon on top. Serves 4.

3. To make white sauce: Melt butter in saucepan over low heat. Blend in flour, salt, and pepper. Add milk all at once. Increase heat and cook quickly, stirring constantly until mixture bubbles and thickens.

Farmer's Omelet

BUCKHORN INN

Attractive, as well as delicious, there is only one way this omelet could be better—waking up at the Buckhorn Inn and having them prepare it for you.

2 tablespoons butter or margarine
2 tablespoons diced onion
1 tablespoon diced green pepper
1 tablespoon diced red pepper
¼ cup sliced mushrooms

2 small red potatoes, boiled and diced
¼ cup diced dill pickle
3 eggs, beaten
2 slices Farmer's cheese

1. In an omelet pan, melt the butter over low heat. Add the onion, green and red pepper, mushrooms, red potatoes, and dill pickle. Saute vegetables over low heat for 5 minutes until they are crisp and tender.

2. Add the eggs. Lift the eggs with a spatula to allow uncooked eggs to run under and cook. When most of the omelet is set, flip, or place under the broiler, (make sure you use an oven-proof pan) to cook the top.

3. Place the cheese on half of the omelet then fold and serve. Makes 2 servings.

Toothpaste works great for removing water stains on wood furniture. Rub paste onto stain with toothbrush. Let dry. Rub off with a damp cloth.

—Buckhorn Inn

Hearty Dutch Omelet

Gil Knier
Heritage Arts

Omelets make a great meal served anytime of day. Try this one at breakfast with hashbrowns and a toasted bagel, or at dinner with a baked potato, steamed asparagus, and a basket of biscuits.

5 eggs
¼ cup sour cream
¼ teaspoon salt
dash of pepper
1 cup fresh, frozen, or canned corn,
    drained

8 ounces hamburger
1 teaspoon butter or margarine
½ to ¾ cup grated Swiss or Monterey
    Jack cheese
dollop of sour cream, optional
dollop of chunky salsa, optional

1. In a large mixing bowl, combine eggs with sour cream, salt, and pepper. Beat until frothy. Stir in corn.

2. In a skillet, brown hamburger. Drain off fat. Remove meat and set aside. Clean skillet and return to stove on medium high heat.

3. Melt butter in skillet. Pour in egg mixture. Cook it omelet style, with a little scrambling, using a spatula. As the eggs begin to set, add the meat, mixing in gently. Sprinkle cheese over eggs and mix lightly. Cook, turning it over once or twice until set. Do not let it get browned. To serve, top with sour cream and salsa. Serves 2.

Variation: Replacing the corn with canned green chiles, and using a mix of cheddar and jack cheese, you can call this a **Hearty Mexican Omelette**. Serve it with **Mexican Green Rice** and hot corn tortillas.

Gateau Fromage

Betty Jane Posey
BETTY JANE POSEY GALLERY

By calling this recipe Gateau Fromage, the men, who say they never eat quiche, may eat this without compromising their manhood. Whether you call this recipe Gateau Fromage or Bacon Quiche, I am sure you will agree it is delicious.

9" baked pie shell	¼ teaspoon salt
8 ounces grated sharp cheddar cheese	⅛ teaspoon pepper
	1 egg, beaten
5 slices bacon	1 tablespoon flour
1 cup sliced onions	¾ cup milk

1. Preheat oven to 400°. Bake and cool pie shell. Place cheese into baked pie shell. Cook bacon until crisp. Remove from pan and drain on paper towel.

2. Saute onions in bacon fat and drain. Put sauteed onions on top of cheese. Crumble bacon and place on top of onions. Sprinkle with salt and pepper. Beat egg, flour, and milk together. Pour into pie without stirring. Bake for 25 to 30 minutes. Serves 4.

Holloway's Country Home

*T*he name of this studio is quite appropriate. Step up onto the porch, open the screen door, and walk into this little country house. It is filled to the brim with quilts, crafts, and gifts. Maria's specialty is making traditional quilts. She also makes quilts using yesterday's patterns worked in today's colors.

A former New Englander, and restaurant owner, Maria is happy with her life as a craftsperson in Tennessee. She and her husband, John, recently opened another quilt and gift studio in a lovely old log cabin in nearby Cosby. With a radiance of peace and contentment, she goes through her twelve hours a day hectic schedule maintaining her calm. She has her own **Recipe for a Happy Life** and shares it in this book.

Maria loves cooking for family gatherings. One time, at a family Christmas in their cabins in Jones Cove, they had 20 guests. For the first two days they had frozen pipes and no water, but Maria was up to the challenge. She found it to be an exciting and memorable occasion with food, fun, and great companionship.

Maria has contributed several fine recipes to this book. Two of my favorites are **Picante Quiche** and **Quilted Rose Seafood Casserole**. Both are quick and easy to prepare and fit right in with a hectic schedule.

Picante Quiche

Maria Holloway
Holloway's Country Home

For breakfast, brunch, lunch, or dinner this recipe is hard to beat for ease, flexibility, and just plain good taste. Try serving it with **Avocado Salad**, tortilla chips, **Chili Roasted New Potatoes**, and fresh steamed asparagus.

½ cup salsa, plus additional ½ cup
6 eggs
1 cup sour cream
1 teaspoon salt

2 teaspoons pepper
¾ cup grated Monterey Jack cheese
¾ cup grated cheddar cheese

1. Preheat oven to 350°. Grease or coat 10" round pie plate with non-stick cooking spray. Spread ½ cup salsa over plate bottom.

2. In a blender, or with mixer, beat eggs and sour cream until frothy. Pour on top of salsa in pie plate. Sprinkle with salt and pepper. Spread cheese on top.

3. Place in oven and bake for 35 to 40 minutes. When done, it will be slightly brown and pulling away from sides of plate. Let it sit 15 minutes before cutting into pie shapes. Serve with additional salsa on top. Fabulous!

Sausage Pie

Vern Hippensteal
Hippensteal Inn

When served with the Hippensteal Inn's **Strawberry Bread**, this is the most popular breakfast combination enjoyed by the guests at this beautiful Inn. The recipe makes two pies, but may be divided in half for a single pie. The next time you have overnight guests, why not surprise them with these two special recipes for breakfast or brunch.

Sausage Pie

2 unbaked pie shells
1 roll of sausage (16 ounces)
6 ounces milk
6 ounces cream
12 ounces sour cream

8 eggs
dash of dry mustard
dash of salt and pepper
4 ounces grated cheese

Pie Shells

2 cups flour
¼ cup cold shortening

ice water

1. Make pie shells or use commercial frozen shells. Cook and drain sausage. Divide into pie shells.

2. Preheat oven to 375°. In a large mixing bowl beat milk, cream, sour cream, eggs, dry mustard, salt, and pepper. Beat well. Divide and pour mixture over sausage. Sprinkle grated cheese on top. Bake for 50 to 60 minutes.

3. To make pie shells: Place flour in mixing bowl. Cut shortening into flour until the size of peas. Pour in enough ice water to form ball out of dough. Divide dough into 2 balls. Wrap in plastic and place in refrigerator for 1 hour. Roll on floured board into 9" pie shells.

Wild Ramps & Scrambled Eggs

Mac McDonell
GEMSTONE

Ramps, a member of the onion family, are legendary in East Tennessee. They even have a Ramps Festival each May in Cosby. Described as the "vilest-smelling, sweetest-tasting weed," this wild leek is purported to be a spring tonic. Mac says the old-timers eat some every year to fight against colds, allergies, and sinuses. Some say it gives your blood a boost after a long winter.

Ramps are three times as strong as garlic. Kids have been sent home from school because teachers and classmates could not tolerate the smell. A waitress in Gatlinburg told me how her Grandma said it would "stink up the whole house, and how Grandpa would spend many a day in the basement with those things and a lot of days in the dog house!"

Ramps are at their strongest when eaten raw, but their potent pungent odor may be tamed by cooking them. They can be fried in fatback and made into gravy, parboiled, added to potato salad, canned and stored. The most popular way to prepare them is with scrambled eggs.

chopped ramps (about ½ cup)	½ teaspoon sugar
fatback	3 eggs, beaten
salt and pepper	

1. To prepare ramps, wash off the bottom of harvested ramps. Peel outside off and trim off roots, like a green onion. Chop the tops and bottoms into small pieces.

2. In a large skillet, fry the fatback, like bacon. Add ramps to hot grease and saute until wilted. Sprinkle with salt, pepper, and sugar (to take the edge off). Add eggs and scramble until eggs are cooked. Serve with biscuits, cornbread, or toast.

Spicy Carrot Souffle

Betty Jane Posey
BETTY JANE POSEY GALLERY

This delightfully spicy souffle would be a great side dish with turkey or chicken, or as the main event for a vegetarian meal. It is at it's best served immediately, but it is still good when reheated!

1 cup mashed cooked carrots (about 5 or 6)
½ cup light brown sugar, packed
¾ teaspoon ginger
¾ teaspoon cinnamon
¼ teaspoon mace

¼ teaspoon salt
1 teaspoon vanilla
3 tablespoons butter, melted
3 tablespoons flour
¾ cup milk
4 eggs, separated

1. In a medium bowl, combine carrots, brown sugar, ginger, cinnamon, mace, salt, and vanilla.

2. In a saucepan, whisk together butter and flour. Add milk and cook over low heat, stirring constantly until thick and smooth. Cool slightly.

3. Beat egg yolks. Add small amount of warm sauce to beaten yolks and mix well. Combine yolks with rest of sauce blending well. Add seasoned carrots to sauce.

4. Preheat oven to 375°. Beat egg whites to form peaks. Carefully fold into carrot mixture. Spoon into 1 ½ quart round casserole, buttered only on bottom. Bake on bottom rack of oven for 45 minutes.

RICE & PASTA

Rice with Almonds & Shallots

Kathy Shields Guttman

This is a great side dish with roast beef or chicken. Add cooked shrimp or scallops and you have a delicious main course.

2 ½ cups water
1 cup long grain rice
1 teaspoon margarine

¼ cup sliced almonds
2 tablespoons diced shallots

1. Bring water to boil in a medium saucepan. Add rice. Cover and cook over medium low heat for 25 minutes.

2. In a small skillet melt margarine. Add sliced almonds and shallots. Saute for about 5 minutes until almonds are golden and shallots are tender. Stir into cooked rice and serve.

"Surround your business with flowers and it will bloom."

—G. Webb
G. Webb Gallery

G's Jumbalaya

G. Webb

G. Webb Gallery

The aroma of this spicy dish (given to the Webbs by a Cajun lady, Mrs. Greene) will fill your kitchen with the scent of New Orleans and turn your thoughts to Mardi Gras. There was something about three beers during the preparation of this recipe that Vicki, G's wife, decided to discretely edit out. However, a frosty cold one (Root Beer or otherwise) would go great with this dish. Bake up a batch of G's **Railroad Tie Biscuits**, fry up some okra, and have a party.

1 cup long grain rice	1 bay leaf
water	½ teaspoon chili powder
2 teaspoons olive oil	½ teaspoon thyme
¾ cup chopped onion	1 tablespoon parsley, chopped
½ cup chopped green pepper	salt and pepper
1 clove garlic, minced	2 cups chicken broth
1 pound smoked sausage, sliced	

1. In a small bowl, soak rice in enough water to cover for 30 minutes. Drain rice.

2. In a large skillet, heat olive oil then add onions, green pepper, garlic, and sausage. Cook over low heat until vegetables are tender. Add rice and stir over low heat until rice is dry.

3. Add bay leaf, chili powder, thyme, parsley, salt, and pepper. Add chicken broth and stir. Cover and cook for 10 to 15 minutes or until rice is tender. Remove bay leaf before serving.

Byrnes Woodcrafters

When you walk into Byrnes Woodcrafters, the scent of cedar fills the air. They make and sell wooden chests, boxes, key rings, toys and, one of their most popular items, cedar wind twisters. A large glass window behind the counter allows you to see the working craftsmen. You might also see Ed Byrnes, owner of this studio.

Originally in the nine to five accounting world for many years, Ed decided he did not want to be doing books and tracking other people's money. He wanted to do something with his own creative talent. With a "special collection of genes kicking around in him" (his mother was an artist, his father an engineer with an MBA, and his grandfather was a carpenter), Ed felt he had what it takes to run a business and showcase his talent to create things. He left the accounting world to start a craft business, and "the rest" he says, "is history."

When not in the studio, or on the golf course, Ed enjoys spending time in the kitchen. His original recipe for **Hillbilly Fried Rice** does a good job of showing off his creative talents.

Hillbilly Fried Rice

Edward Byrnes
Byrnes Woodcrafters

This is an excellent side dish with a hot zesty flavor. Add chicken, beef, or shrimp and you have a main course. Ed says "This is a great recipe to serve with any Mexican food or a bowl of chili. Mucho bueno, ya'll!"

1 ½ cups minute rice
1 ½ cups water
1 teaspoon margarine or butter
2 tablespoons olive oil
1 clove garlic, minced (or garlic salt)

fresh or frozen okra
10 ounce can diced tomatoes with green chiles
½ teaspoon paprika
hot pepper sauce to taste

1. Cook minute rice in large sauce pan or skillet per package instructions with water and margarine.

2. In same skillet, when rice is done, add olive oil, garlic, okra, diced tomatoes with green chiles, paprika, and hot sauce. Cook over medium high heat to fry the rice, mixing and turning as needed. Serves 6.

To remove scotch tape or any tape residue, use WD40. It dissolves the glue effortlessly, especially on windows.

—Edward Byrnes
Byrnes Woodcrafters

Earthspeak

*T*his studio, described as a fine art gallery, workshop, and old style trading post, is a delight to the eyes as well as the senses. Beautifully displayed Native American, natural, and mystical arts and crafts are the primary focus of its member artisans.

Karen Pierre, whose work includes incredibly intricate and detailed drawings of animals and the spiritual/mystical world, offers these words: "As we developed the concept for our shop, we realized the turtle, the oldest Native American symbol for Mother Earth, was perfect for Earthspeak. Our goal is to share positive experiences as we relearn to accept the abundance which surrounds us. We know we must once again act as stewards of the Earth, protecting our home and honoring all life. To the many people who come to this area who share our views of the Earth, and our deep love of the Smoky Mountains, we offer our love and respect."

Gregg Culley of Earthspeak, a seventh generation basketmaker and aficionado of southwestern cuisine, offers his recipe for **Mexican Green Rice.**

Mexican Green Rice

Gregg Culley
EARTHSPEAK

Gregg is a seventh generation basketmaker. His specialty is making traditional Appalachian baskets, Cherokee River Cone baskets, and Navajo Dream Catchers. When not in Gatlinburg, he spends time in New Mexico developing his craft and enjoying the tastes of southwestern cooking.

His recipe for Mexican Green Rice can be made as hot or mild as you like by adjusting the variety of mild or hot peppers. This rice makes a wonderful side dish with cheese enchiladas or chili rellenos.

boiling water	3 to 6 pablano peppers, finely chopped
1 cup long grain rice	2 jalapeno peppers, finely chopped
1 tablespoon vegetable oil	2 green peppers, chopped
1 to 2 onions, finely chopped	2 tablespoons chopped fresh cilantro
2 cups chicken broth	

1. Pour enough boiling water to cover raw rice (this gives rice a nice texture). Let sit 30 minutes. Drain until dry.

2. Coat skillet with vegetable oil. On medium heat, add rice and onions to skillet. Cook until rice is brownish yellow. Add chicken broth, peppers, and cilantro. Cover and cook rice for about 20 minutes on medium low heat until it reaches desired tenderness.

Pilau Rice

Mary Louise Hunt
FIBER CREATIONS INC.

This wonderfully fragrant rice dish may be the central part of a vegetarian meal, or a perfect side dish for grilled fresh salmon or rainbow trout.

5 tablespoons butter	¼ teaspoon chili powder
1 medium onion, chopped	2 teaspoons mustard seeds
½ cup raisins	¼ teaspoon cardamom powder
1 tablespoon pine nuts or almonds	1 ½ cups rice
2 teaspoons salt	3 ¾ cups hot water

1. Melt butter in saucepan. Saute onion, raisins, nuts, salt, chili powder, mustard seeds, and cardamom powder for 5 minutes. Add rice and continue to saute over low heat, stirring frequently, for 7 minutes.

2. Pour water over rice, cover and cook over low heat until rice is done, approximately 15 minutes.

Note: Mustard seeds and cardamom powder may not be part of your normal spice pantry. You may wish to buy these spices in small quantities. The best place to do that is at a bulk food outlet.

Rice and Corn Chicken

Gil Knier
Heritage Arts

This casserole may be made into a soup by adding more water or milk, plus another can of corn. Gil likes to serve this hearty dish with corn bread and fruit salad. Leftovers may be reheated the next day.

1 chicken, cut up
2 quarts water
2 tablespoons salt
1 teaspoon pepper
¼ teaspoon ginger
sage, to taste

2 ½ cups uncooked long grain rice
1 medium can corn niblets
1 can cream of mushroom soup
1 cup diced celery or frozen mixed
  vegetables

1. In a large pot, place the chicken, water, salt, pepper, ginger, and sage. Bring to a boil. Cover and reduce to a simmer. Cook until chicken is tender (about 1 ½ hours).

2. Remove chicken from pot, allow to cool, then debone and skin. Return meat to broth. Add rice, corn, mushroom soup, and vegetables. Stir to blend. Cover and allow to simmer until rice is done, about 30 minutes.

Franks Go Around Supper

Joan Royer
BUNNIES N BEARS BY JOAN

Here is a dressed up version of every child's favorite macaroni and cheese dinner. This is easy and fun to do, so why not let the kids make it. Making it themselves, maybe they will actually eat the vegetables.

2 packages 7 ¼ ounce macaroni
    dinner mix
1 cup chopped onion
½ cup chopped green peppers
2 tablespoons margarine

1 cup shredded carrots
1 teaspoon Worcestershire sauce
½ teaspoon sage
8 franks (hot dogs) split

1. Preheat oven to 350°. Grease a 2 quart casserole. In a saucepan, prepare macaroni dinners as directed on package, except using ⅔ cup of milk.

2. Saute onion and peppers in margarine. Add to cooked macaroni with carrots, Worcestershire sauce, and sage. Mix.

3. Line greased casserole with franks. Spoon macaroni mixture into center. Cover with foil. Bake for 35 minutes. If desired, garnish with green pepper rings. Serves 8.

Aunt Carla (Beef and Macaroni Casserole)

Gena Lewis
Lewis Family Crafts

This hearty concoction was given to Gena from her sister-in-law, Carla McDowell. She threw it together one time and now it is a favorite of the whole clan. A visiting niece asked what it was called. No one had a good name for it so she coined it Aunt Carla.

1 ½ pounds lean ground beef	1 can corn, drained
16 ounce can tomato sauce	2 ½ cups dry macaroni
1 package taco seasoning	1 cup grated cheddar cheese

1. In a large skillet, cook beef until well browned and crumbled. Add tomato sauce, taco seasoning, and canned corn. Cook on medium heat while preparing macaroni.

2. In a large pot of boiling water, cook macaroni until al dente. Drain well.

3. Mix cooked macaroni with meat mixture and pour into a 9" x 13" baking dish. Sprinkle cheese on top and bake at 350° for 25 minutes.

"My Mom was a simple cook, yet she knew how to make everything taste good. She taught me how to improvise when out of something, and what staples to keep on hand, so you can always make something. I learned how to cook large amounts of everything. Mom cooked for 10 kids, and Dad ate like four more. It took me years to make lemon pies and bread like Mom's. She taught me more than how to cook, she taught me how to eat healthy."

—Gena Lewis
Lewis Family Crafts

Goulash Italiano

Gil Knier
HERITAGE ARTS

This is a great make-ahead dish for a casual party or family gathering. The flavors have a chance to intensify when made earlier in the day, or the previous night. Gil sometimes replaces the mushrooms with chopped, peeled tomatoes, and tops the goulash with grated mozzarella cheese.

1 pound lean ground beef
2 cups chunky-style vegetable spaghetti sauce
1 can cream of mushroom soup
2 cups sliced mushrooms
1 tablespoon sugar
½ teaspoon salt
¼ teaspoon pepper
garlic powder
1 tablespoon vegetable oil
12 ounce package wide egg noodles
grated mozzarella cheese, optional

1. In a large skillet, brown ground beef. Drain off the fat and discard. Add spaghetti sauce and cream of mushroom soup. Mix well. Add mushrooms, sugar (to cut the acidity of tomato sauce), salt, pepper, and several dashes of garlic powder. Cook over low heat for 25 minutes.

2. Add vegetable oil to a large pot of boiling water. Cook egg noodles according to package directions. Drain the noodles in a colander and return them to the pot. Add the meat sauce and stir to blend. Allow to simmer for 5 to 10 minutes, stirring occasionally. Sprinkle with mozzarella cheese, if desired, before serving.

Pasta Casserole

Victoria Azpurua
HOMESPUN HEART

When you are in the mood for some real "comfort food," try this tantalizing casserole, chock full of cheese. This is a great make-ahead dish for a pot-luck with friends.

1 ½ pounds lean ground beef
1 onion, diced
1 bell pepper, diced
1 jar mushrooms, or 1 pound fresh,
    sliced
1 can sliced black olives, drained
1 large jar spaghetti sauce

¼ teaspoon garlic powder
½ teaspoon Italian seasoning
½ teaspoon oregano
16 ounce box pasta
16 ounce package sharp cheddar
    cheese, cut in chunks

1. In a large frying pan, brown ground beef. Drain grease. Add onion and bell pepper. Cook until vegetables are slightly tender (approximately 4 to 5 minutes). Add mushrooms, black olives, spaghetti sauce, and seasonings. Let simmer on low heat for 10 minutes.

2. Cook pasta according to package directions. Drain well. Mix the pasta in with the sauce. Mix ⅔'s of the cheese chunks into the pasta. Place mixture in a lightly greased 9" x 13" casserole. Sprinkle remaining chunks evenly over top. Bake at 375° for 30 minutes.

When you are cutting up onions, to rid yourself of the "onion smell," hold a stainless steel fork or spoon and run your hands under cold water.

—Victoria Azpurua
Homespun Heart

Baked Spaghetti

Sara Kane

ADOUGHABLE THINGS BY NANCY

Sara works at Adoughable Things by Nancy, and Shucks Y'all. She lost about 75 pounds on Weight Watchers, and has successfully maintained her weight loss for many years.

Her recipe for Baked Spaghetti is a cross between spaghetti and lasagna. Dieters and non-dieters alike will enjoy this low calorie dish. It is even better re-heated the next day.

1 egg, beaten	¼ cup chopped onions
8 ounces spaghetti noodles, cooked	1 cup sliced mushrooms
4 teaspoons margarine	2 cups spaghetti sauce
¾ ounces Parmesan cheese	½ teaspoon Italian seasonings
salt and pepper	garlic powder to taste
½ pound ground beef	1 ⅓ cups non-fat cottage cheese
¼ cup chopped green peppers	3 ounces grated mozzarella cheese

1. Coat a 9" x 13" pan with non-stick oil spray. Preheat oven to 350°. In a large bowl, mix together egg, cooked spaghetti, margarine, Parmesan cheese, salt, and pepper. Spread mixture evenly over prepared pan.

2. Brown ground beef and drain fat. Add green peppers, onions, and mushrooms. Saute together with beef. Add spaghetti sauce, Italian seasonings, and garlic powder.

3. Spread cottage cheese over noodles. Pour sauce over cheese. Bake for 30 minutes. Sprinkle mozzarella cheese on top and bake another 10 minutes until cheese melts. Remove from oven and let set 10 minutes before serving.

Spaghetti for a Crowd

Cecil Posey
BETTY JANE POSEY GALLERY

"We're going to be open tonight with Cecil's spaghetti," read the sign in the window of the Owl's Nest Restaurant. The Poseys owned it during their early years in Gatlinburg. Mostly opened for breakfast and lunch only, when that sign was posted, a huge crowd showed up for dinner.

2 tablespoons olive oil
6 large onions, chopped
5 large green peppers, chopped
3 cloves garlic, finely chopped
4 pounds lean ground beef
1 small can chili powder
salt and pepper
1 teaspoon oregano
1 large can tomatoes

2 large cans tomato soup
1 jar pimento
½ cup butter
1 pound beef sausage, cubed or sliced
1 quart water
1 large can mushrooms, drained
1 large can ripe olives, drained
4 fresh tomatoes, chopped

1. In a large pot, heat olive oil. Saute onions, green peppers, and garlic until golden. In a separate skillet, brown beef with chili powder, salt, pepper, and oregano. Drain grease and add meat to vegetables.

2. Add canned tomatoes, tomato soup, pimentos, butter, beef sausage, and water. Simmer at least 2 to 3 hours. Add mushrooms, olives, and fresh tomatoes. Simmer for another hour. Serve with pasta. Sauce freezes well.

"I used my mother's recipe. I use fresh hamburger meat and tomatoes, the regular spaghetti ingredients, but we cooked it the right way. Drain the grease off, let it simmer…"

—Cecil Posey
The Betty Jane Posey Gallery

Cosby Hillpeople Crafts

Carl Fogliani, originally from south of the Mason-Dixon line in Kentucky, and his wife, Libby, a native of the Smokies, started doing crafts in 1981, but did not open their Gatlinburg studio until 1991. When not in the studio, or out doing eight craft shows a year, they spend time in the woods gathering fresh berries and fruit for their homemade jellies, and pine cones and grapevines for making wreaths. They have quite a range of crafts. Everything from birdfeeders, mailboxes, and wreaths, to applique and tied quilts, toys, Christmas ornaments, and novelties.

If Carl ever gets tired of the craft business, he should be a stand-up comedian. With his deep voice, a dead-pan look on his face, and a twinkle in his eyes, he goes into a humorous routine when customers come in and pick up one of his novelty items. I am told he draws quite a crowd at craft shows when he demonstrates his Gatlinburg Table Tennis Ball Guns, one of his most popular novelties.

When he gets the chance, Carl enjoys cooking. He has developed his own special recipes for hushpuppies and lasagna. Carl says the first step in preparing his lasagna is "going to the bank and taking out a loan." It takes a fair amount of time and ingredients, but it is worth it.

Carl's Lasagna

Carl Fogliani
Cosby Hillpeople Crafts

This is Carl's original recipe. I have given you the instructions for it in his own words. Did I mention Carl has a good sense of humor? It took me a couple of times reading over the instructions to get the wine right. Three glasses (4 ounces each) go in the sauce and you drink 3 glasses (optional, of course). By the time you are finished cooking, both you and the sauce will be nice and mellow.

Plan ahead when making this dish. The sauce should be made the day before the lasagna. You may eat the lasagna the day you make it, or prepare it and serve it the next day.

Lasagna Sauce

red wine	8 ounces sliced fresh mushrooms
2 tablespoons olive oil	½ cup chopped green olives
1 pound ground beef	2 tablespoons oregano (1 plus 1)
salt and pepper	2 cups crushed tomatoes
4 cloves garlic, chopped (2 plus 2)	2 cups stewed Italian style tomatoes
1 large onion, chopped	1 cup tomato juice
1 large green pepper, chopped	

1. Pour 2 glasses of wine. Pour olive oil in a large dutch oven. Heat on low. Crumble meat into bottom of pot. Add salt and pepper to taste along with 2 cloves of garlic, onion, green pepper, mushrooms, olives, and second glass of wine. You are supposed to be drinking the first glass.

2. Pour 2 more glasses of wine. Add 1 tablespoon of oregano. Stir and cover. Let simmer until vegetables are tender, about 15 minutes. Add fourth glass of wine. You should be on your second glass by now.

3. Pour 2 more glasses of wine. Add 2 more cloves of garlic and 1 tablespoon of oregano. Add crushed tomatoes, stewed tomatoes, tomato juice, and last glass of wine. That's right, you should be drinking your third glass.

4. Let sauce cook down over low heat about 3 to 4 hours. Stir occasionally to avoid sticking or burning. If you pace yourself, you will finish the bottle of wine when the

sauce is done. Let sauce sit overnight. Reheat next day to prepare lasagna. This also goes well with spaghetti noodles. Sauce freezes well.

Lasagna

¼ teaspoon salt
1 teaspoon olive oil
1 package lasagna noodles
Carl's lasagna sauce
oregano
1 cup grated Parmesan cheese

1 cup grated Romano cheese
1 container ricotta cheese
24 ounces shredded mozzarella
  cheese
12 ounce package sliced Provolone
  cheese

1. Bring large pot of water to boil. Add salt and olive oil. Cook noodles until tender (about 12 to 15 minutes). Drain and run cold water over noodles. Drain well.

2. Preheat oven to 350°. Grease a deep dish pan (14" x 10" x 3") with olive oil. Spread 1 ½ to 2 cups of sauce over bottom of pan. Sprinkle with oregano. Cover with layer of noodles. Sprinkle with some Parmesan and Romano cheese. Add a large scoop of ricotta and spread with spoon. Cover with some of the mozzarella. Place a layer of Provolone cheese on mozzarella. Repeat procedure with sauce, then noodles, then cheeses to fill pan.

3. Finish top layer of pan with sauce. Sprinkle with Parmesan and Romano cheese. Place in oven for about 30 minutes. Makes 6 to 8 generous servings. Reheats well.

DESSERTS, CAKES, & PIES

Angel Food Surprise

Gena Lewis
LEWIS FAMILY CRAFTS

Gena likes to keep this in a Tupperware container in the freezer for a quick summer dessert. This cool treat came from her sister-in-law, Carolyn Lewis.

1 angel food cake
1 quart sherbet, softened

8 ounces frozen whipped topping, defrosted

1. Slice angel food cake horizontally to make 3 layers.

2. Spread half of sherbet on bottom layer, like you were icing a cake. Put middle cake layer on top and put remaining sherbet on it. Put on top layer of cake.

3. Spread whipped topping on sides, top, and down the center of cake. Freeze for a few hours before serving. May be covered in plastic wrap once frozen, or placed in a Tupperware container.

Being on a lowfat diet, I have learned to substitute fats in recipes. For cakes and baked goods, substitute fat with applesauce. Use egg substitutes instead of eggs. You will save fat and cholesterol. Use herbs and spices for flavor.

—Gena Lewis
Lewis Family Crafts

Cherry Jubilee

Wilma Prebor
QUILTS BY WILMA

Wilma's sister gave her this recipe. Since you make this recipe the day before serving, this creamy cool no-bake dessert is perfect for company dinners on hot summer days.

1 box vanilla wafers, crushed
½ cup butter, softened
1 ½ cups powdered sugar

2 eggs
1 can cherry pie filling
1 cup heavy cream, whipped

1. Lightly butter a 9" x 13" glass baking pan. Spread half of crushed wafers evenly over bottom. Cream butter and powdered sugar until fluffy. Beat eggs in, one at a time. Beat well until it looks like whipped cream. Spread carefully over wafers.

2. Spread cherry pie filling carefully on top of butter mixture. Whip cream and spread over cherries. Sprinkle remaining crushed wafers on top of whipped cream. Let sit in refrigerator over night before serving.

"Every quilt is a piece of art work. You can give the same pattern to 10 people and come back with 10 entirely different quilts. Due to the amount of one's self put into the quilt, not just the time, but artistic ability, it becomes part of one's life."

—Wilma Prebor
Quilts by Wilma

Cranberry/Raspberry Delight

Maria Holloway
HOLLOWAY'S COUNTRY HOME

Maria says this is a great treat served with any entree, but especially good with turkey. You may serve this as a molded salad with your meal, or as a dessert.

Gelatin mold

1 large box raspberry gelatin
 (6 serving size)
15 ounce can whole cranberry sauce

15 ounce can crushed pineapple
¾ cup crushed walnuts

Sour cream yogurt dressing

½ cup sour cream
½ cup plain yogurt

1 tablespoon almond extract

1. Prepare gelatin according to package directions, but eliminate ½ cup boiling water. Add cranberry sauce and stir to dissolve. Add crushed pineapple and walnuts. Stir.

2. Pour into individual molds, or one large mold. If not available, pour into a large round casserole. Set in refrigerator overnight. Serve individual portions topped with dressing.

3. To prepare dressing, combine sour cream, yogurt, and almond extract. For a sweeter dressing, use vanilla yogurt or add a teaspoon of sugar.

"A great way to make a living is doing what one loves, working 12-hour days and liking it."

—Maria Holloway
Holloway's Country Home

Jello Shocker

John Thomas
Pewter by Hedko

On a hot summer day, when the humidity is high, and it feels like 105° in the shade, your appetite leans towards light and refreshing. John's Jello Shocker is just the dish to cool you down. In fact, you may be tempted to skip dinner and go straight to a double helping of dessert.

¾ cup boiling water
3 ounce box of Wild Strawberry
    gelatin
1 cup ice cubes

1 ripe banana
½ cup frozen whipped topping,
    defrosted

1. Pour boiling water into blender and add gelatin. Blend on low speed until mixed (about 30 seconds). Add ice cubes and stir with spoon until cubes are almost completely melted. Remove unmelted pieces of ice.

2. Add banana and whipped topping. Blend on high speed until smooth (another 30 seconds). Pour into dessert cups and refrigerate until set. Serves 4 to 6.

Customer Loyalty

As any craftsman, artist, or tradesman can attest, customer loyalty is the greatest endorsement and affirmation in ones work. Here is just such an example: From Kalamazoo, Michigan, Miriam and Bob were down to the Smokies for their semi-annual visit when Bob decided that a slight discomfort was just enough to have him visit a doctor. After all, some of their hikes tended to be long and into remote areas.

Bob's little persistent, hardly worth-it, tenderness, turned out to be a ruptured appendix! Miriam reports that as the anesthesia was taking effect, Bob looked up from the gurney (speeding down the corridor to surgery) to say, "But we haven't been to the pewter shop yet." Not only did they make a visit to my pewter shop, they extended their vacation a few days as well.

—John Thomas
Pewter by Hedko

The Leather Works

*T*his studio makes and sells a wide variety of handcrafted leather items, everything from belts and wallets to intricately detailed leather saddles. Just about any leather item you want you will be able to find there, or have custom made.

Annetta Hendrickson and Pat Wills of The Leather Works are two examples of craftspeople who are creative in the kitchen. I had mouth watering conversations with both of them on interesting ways to prepare food. Annetta and I discussed some new spins on old country cooking; and Pat had some innovative ideas on homemade ice cream and the many uses of Anise oil.

Try Annetta's recipe for **Cornish Hens with Rice**. It makes an elegant meal without much fuss. And, for dessert, have a big bowl of Pat's **Home Coming Ice Cream**. After all that rich dining, prepare a pot of Annetta's **Pinto Beans & Dumplings**.

Home Coming Ice Cream

Pat Wills
THE LEATHER WORKS

Pat makes this for his annual church picnic. His advice is "save some for yourself, it is usually gone within 10 minutes of serving."

Pat uses an old-fashioned ice cream churn purchased years ago from Wal-Mart and starts with the basic vanilla ice cream recipe that came with the churn. I looked high and low for an old fashioned churn to test the recipe, but was unable to find one. So I adapted Pat's recipe to use commercial ice cream. However, if you are lucky enough to have an ice cream churn, use your favorite vanilla ice cream recipe and add the candy and oil of anise just before churning.

1 gallon vanilla ice cream
12 ounces chocolate covered brickle bits

12 ounces mini chocolate chips
¼ to ½ teaspoon oil of anise

1. Soften ice cream and mix in brickle bits, chocolate chips, and oil of anise (a little bit goes a long way. Add a little and taste before adding more).

Note: If you are not serving a crowd, just adjust the amount of the above ingredients to as much vanilla ice cream as you like.

"Cades Cove is like a trip back in time, you can almost feel you were one of the first settlers."

—Annetta Hendrickson
Leather Works

Lowfat Cheesecake

Gena Lewis
LEWIS FAMILY CRAFTS

Found from desperation while dieting, Gena says this is one of her best recipes. She modified a recipe she found for cheesecake by using fat-free ingredients and cutting down the sugar by using an artificial sweetener.

This recipe is going to make a lot of dieters and people watching their cholesterol very happy. No one will know that this is a diet version of cheesecake. It is creamy and delicious. Serve it plain or with sliced fruit, fresh raspberries, or a canned fruit topping.

¼ cup graham cracker crumbs
16 ounces fat-free cream cheese
1 ¾ to 2 cups plain yogurt cheese
    (recipe follows)
1 cup sugar (or half sugar & half
    artificial sweetener)
⅔ cup egg substitute
2 teaspoons vanilla
1 teaspoon grated lemon peel
1 tablespoon lemon juice

1. Preheat oven to 350°. Coat a 9" springform pan with non-stick spray. Sprinkle bottom with graham cracker crumbs. Refrigerate.

2. Beat cream cheese until smooth. Add yogurt cheese and beat well. Gradually beat in sugar. Add egg substitute, vanilla, lemon peel, and lemon juice. Beat until smooth. Pour into springform pan.

3. Bake 50 to 60 minutes until edges are set. Place shallow pan of hot water on lower rack to avoid cracking. Remove from oven. When cool, remove sides of pan and refrigerate. If desired, serve with topping.

4. To make Yogurt Cheese: Line colander with coffee filters. Allow 1 quart of lowfat plain or vanilla yogurt to drain in refrigerator overnight. Consistency will be like cream cheese. This is also great for dips or spreads.

Mud Pie

The Buckhorn Inn

I now understand the name of this dessert. When you mix the melted butter with the Oreo cookie crumbs, it looks like mud. It brought back memories long ago of making mud pies in my backyard—only this time everybody wanted to eat it. This recipe gets my vote for one of the best tasting, easiest, impressive, and fun to make desserts.

1 pound Oreo cookies
1 cup butter, melted
½ gallon vanilla ice cream

½ gallon coffee ice cream
10 to 12 ounces chocolate fudge sauce
sliced almonds

1. Finely crush cookies in a food processor, or in plastic bag with a mallet. In a mixing bowl, combine the crumbs with the melted butter. Line the bottom and sides of an 11" springform pan with the crumb mixture. Place in freezer for 30 minutes.

2. In a large mixing bowl combine the ice creams and allow to soften. Blend until smooth. Fill the cookie-lined pan with the ice cream. Freeze for at least 2 hours.

3. Remove pie from freezer. Pour fudge sauce on top. Sprinkle with almonds. Freeze for at least 1 hour before serving. Serves 8 to 10.

"Some of our favorite places in the Smokies are Greenbrier swimming holes—ask us for directions to secret spots."

—Buckhorn Inn

Pineapple Salad

Donna Baxter
BAXTER'S STAINED GLASS

This recipe was a solid hit at a taste-testing dinner party. Even people who normally do not like nuts or marshmallows in anything, admitted this dish was great as they scooped up their second helping.

14 ounce can pineapple chunks,
    drained
3 tablespoons sugar
2 tablespoons flour
1 tablespoon butter

2 egg yolks
¼ cup nuts
12 large marshmallows, cut up
3 bananas, sliced

1. Drain juice from pineapple. Place juice in small saucepan. Add sugar, flour, butter, and egg yolks. Whisk together. Cook over low heat until thickened.

2. In a medium bowl, pour warm liquid dressing over pineapple. When cool, add nuts, marshmallows, and bananas. Refrigerate before serving.

Note: To make it easy to cut marshmallows, spread margarine on the blade of a knife.

"Grotto Falls, Laurel Falls, and Cades Cove are some of our favorite places in the Smokies. Our favorite meals are spur of the moment picnics in the Park after we close the shop for the day. We take anything we happen to have and go. Sometimes it is even hot soup in a thermos."

—Donna Baxter
Baxter's Stained Glass

Frozen Pineapple Salad

Gena Lewis
LEWIS FAMILY CRAFTS

After tasting this delightfully creamy frozen treat, my young Canadian friend Tim (5 years old) decided he loved the salad and wanted to be one of my official Tennessee Taste Testers.

8 ounces fat-free cream cheese
¼ cup fat-free mayonnaise
8 ounces light frozen whipped
    topping, defrosted

½ pound marshmallows
1 small can crushed pineapple

1. In a large bowl, cream together the cream cheese and mayonnaise. Fold in whipped topping. Gently fold in marshmallows and pineapple.

2. Pour into a lightly greased 10-cup bundt pan or large mold. Freeze for at least 5 hours.

"My hobbies are all family oriented. I paint oils and watercolor landscapes and old buildings. I also collect cookbooks, but I have a rule of thumb. I don't buy a cookbook unless it has at least one good recipe in it. My other passion (besides my husband) is genealogy and historical facts (you can't have one without the other)."

—Gena Lewis
Lewis Family Crafts

Betty Jane Posey Gallery

Walking into Betty Jane's studio is like walking into a candy store, it is almost impossible to choose just one favorite to take home. Watercolors and oils depicting Smoky Mountain scenes and beautiful florals of roses, dogwoods, pansies, and petunias line the walls. Paintings depicting Victorian style southern homes and gardens share with the viewer a glimpse of her past growing up in Georgia. Her paintings, all original, are handsomely framed by her husband Cecil.

"Food and art have always been part of our life," says Betty Jane. "Poverty led to food, food led to a restaurant and the restaurant led to art." Having learned the art of cooking delicious and nutritious meals on next to no money, they opened a restaurant.

The walls were decorated with her paintings on barnboard. She handpainted menu covers and drew pictures on the customers checks. When people started buying her art off the wall, requesting her autograph on their menu, and taking their check home to frame, she began to think "maybe there is a talent here." After a decision to sell the restaurant, she made up her mind to paint. She has been painting professionally now for over 25 years. Her work is collected by people across North America, England, and Australia.

Betty Jane has contributed many fine recipes to this book. Like her paintings, it is impossible for me to choose my favorite one. They are all great.

WHOP BISCUITS & FRIED APPLE PIE

Really Easy Peach Cobbler

Betty Jane Posey
BETTY JANE POSEY GALLERY

When it comes to simple and good cooking, Betty Jane is a master. Her peach cobbler is really easy and really good. When fresh peaches are in season, do not miss trying this recipe.

⅓ cup butter
1 cup sugar, plus ½ to 1 cup
¾ cup flour
2 teaspoons baking powder

dash of salt
¾ cup milk
2 cups sliced fresh peaches

1. Preheat oven to 350°. Lightly grease a deep round casserole dish. Melt butter in casserole.

2. In a separate bowl, mix 1 cup of the sugar, flour, baking powder, salt, and milk. Pour batter into middle of the melted butter. Do not stir.

3. Mix peaches with the remaining sugar (½ to 1 cup depending on how sweet you want it) and pour into middle of the batter. Do not stir. Bake 1 hour. May be served hot or cold.

Variation: By adding a handful of fresh raspberries to this recipe and serving it with a scoop of vanilla ice cream you will create a **Peach Melba Cobbler**.

"I will never be able to retire from being an artist, for it is an integral part of my life, a delightful and wonderful gift. Each painting is special and is an attempt to reach out to the one person who will own that painting in a most personal way. Each painting is a part of me, directly from my mind's concept, from my heart, and from my hand."

—Betty Jane Posey
Betty Jane Posey Gallery

Spiced Pear

Dave Howard
Spiced Pear Cafe

This is the Spiced Pear Cafe's signature dessert. It consists of fresh Burgundy poached pears served with a white chocolate ganache. Dave uses the finest quality Callebaut white chocolate to prepare the rich creamy ganache.

This is a good make-ahead dessert. The pears keep well in the poaching liquid for up to three weeks, and the ganache may be made ahead. The longer the pears rest in the liquid, the more intense becomes the color of the pear. The poaching liquid may be used again to cook additional pears.

Pears

6 Bosc pears	1 teaspoon vanilla
1 bottle Burgundy wine	2 cups water
2 cinnamon sticks	4 cups sugar

White chocolate ganache

6 ounces white chocolate	½ cup heavy cream

1. Peel pears. Do not remove stem. With a melon baller, carefully remove core of seeds from pear.

2. In a large pot combine Burgundy, cinnamon sticks, vanilla, water, and sugar. Heat and mix well to blend and dissolve sugar. Place pears in liquid and bring to a boil. Boil for 15 minutes until pears begin to darken. Reduce heat and simmer for 10 minutes. Remove from heat and allow pears to cool in liquid.

3. To serve, place a large dollop of warm ganache on individual plate and place heated pear on top (Dave warms sauce in microwave just until it begins to bubble, less than 30 seconds for individual serving, and heats the pear in microwave until steaming, about 1 minute per pear).

4. To prepare ganache: melt white chocolate with cream in double boiler. Whisk well to blend. Allow to sit and thicken.

Raw Apple Cake

Gena Lewis
Lewis Family Crafts

Apple pie, apple cakes, apple squares, applesauce, I love them all. The only problem with most apple recipes is that you have to peel the apples. I hate peeling apples. I find it boring and tedious. The juice is always flying up and coating my eyeglasses. But, I do it frequently because the finished product is always worth it.

Gena's Raw Apple Cake is the perfect apple dessert for those of you like myself who hate peeling apples. All you do is clean, core, and chop—what could be easier! The taste and texture of this cake is unbeatable. You may use any of your favorite nuts for this recipe, but try using hazelnuts, they really compliment the apples.

3 eggs	3 cups flour
2 cups sugar	1 teaspoon vanilla
1 ½ cups vegetable oil	4 cups chopped apples, do not peel
1 teaspoon baking soda	1 cup nuts, chopped
1 teaspoon cinnamon	

1. Preheat oven to 325°. With mixer, beat eggs, sugar, and oil until well blended. Mix together baking soda, cinnamon, and flour. Stir into sugar mixture.

2. Add vanilla, apples, and nuts. Stir until evenly mixed. Batter will be very thick. Spread into a 9" x 13" ungreased pan. Bake for 40 to 45 minutes. Good plain or with ice cream or whipped topping.

Blueberry Cinnamon Crumb Cake

Kathy Shields Guttman

This is a summertime favorite in our home when blueberries are in season. I sometimes substitute fresh diced peaches for the blueberries.

1 cup sugar
2 ¼ cups flour
1 teaspoon cinnamon
¾ cup butter, cut in 1" chunks
1 teaspoon baking soda
1 cup sour cream

2 eggs, beaten
1 teaspoon vanilla
1 teaspoon baking powder
1 ¼ cups blueberries
additional cinnamon

1. Preheat oven to 375°. Grease and flour an 8" x 8" or 7" x 11" baking pan. In a large mixing bowl, combine sugar, flour, cinnamon, and butter (in small chunks). Cut mixture with pastry blender, or knives, until it is the texture of fine crumbs. Measure and remove 1 cup of crumbs and set aside.

2. Dissolve baking soda in sour cream and add to remaining flour mixture. Add beaten eggs, vanilla, and baking powder. Stir until well mixed. Fold blueberries into batter.

3. Pour into prepared pan. Sprinkle reserved crumbs on top. Sprinkle with additional cinnamon. Bake for 35 to 45 minutes. Cake freezes well.

To grease cake pans, mix twice as much solid shortening with flour. Store and use as needed.

—Sara Kane
Adoughable Things

Bobbie's Carrot Cake

Bobbie Adams
ADAMS MILL

Don and Bobbie Adams recently closed their craft shop in Florida and moved to Gatlinburg. They now share studio space with Maria Holloway at Holloway's Country Home. Don is a wood craftsman and Bobbie is an artist who works in various mediums and styles.

Her style of carrot cake is dense and not overly sweet and oily as some carrot cakes. The icing, however, adds all the sweetness and rich taste you could possibly want. My panel of taste-testers gave it a thumbs-up!

Carrot cake

3 cups sifted flour
1 teaspoon baking powder
1 teaspoon baking soda
½ teaspoon salt
3 teaspoons cinnamon

¾ cup oil
1 cup sugar
4 eggs
4 cups grated carrots (about 8 large)

Cream cheese icing

¼ cup margarine, softened
8 ounces cream cheese, softened

16 ounces powdered sugar
1 teaspoon vanilla

1. Preheat oven to 350°. Grease and flour three 8" round cake pans. Sift flour, baking powder, baking soda, salt, and cinnamon together. Set aside.

2. Cream oil and sugar together. Beat in eggs one at a time. Gradually beat in flour mixture. Add carrots. Mix well. Pour batter into pans. Bake for 25 to 30 minutes. Cool. Spread icing on each layer and then on top and sides of cake. Chill before serving.

3. To prepare icing: Cream margarine and cream cheese. Add sugar and vanilla. Beat until smooth.

Coconut Cake

Vern Hippensteal
Hippensteal Inn

Big, beautiful, moist, and delicious describes this cake. Because it is made three days before serving, it is the perfect make-ahead dessert for a dinner party or holiday meal.

1 box butter or white cake mix
1 ¾ cups sugar
16 ounces sour cream

12 ounces thawed frozen coconut (or packaged, not frozen)
6 ounces frozen whipped topping, defrosted

1. Prepare cake mix according to directions, making two 8" layers. When completely cool, split both layers.

2. Combine sugar, sour cream, and coconut. Chill. Reserve 1 cup sour cream mixture for frosting. Spread remainder between layers.

3. Combine reserved sour cream mixture with whipped topping and frost cake. Seal in airtight container. Refrigerate 3 days before serving.

$300 Chocolate Cake

Wilma Prebor
QUILTS BY WILMA

Honestly, this cake does not cost $300 to make. However, it is a rich chocolate cake, topped with a luscious rich cocoa icing.

Cake

2 cups sugar	½ cup buttermilk
2 cups flour	1 teaspoon baking soda
1 cup water	2 eggs
½ cup butter	dash of salt
¾ cup vegetable oil	1 teaspoon vanilla
¼ cup cocoa	

Cocoa icing

¼ cup cocoa	1 teaspoon vanilla
½ cup butter	16 ounces powdered sugar
¼ cup milk	

1. Preheat oven to 350°. Grease and flour a 9" x 13" baking pan.

2. In a large mixing bowl, combine sugar and flour. In a saucepan, bring water, butter, vegetable oil, and cocoa to a boil. Cook for 1 minute, stirring constantly. Pour cooked mixture over sugar and flour. Stir well. Add buttermilk, baking soda, eggs, salt, and vanilla. Stir well.

3. Pour into prepared pan. Bake for 40 minutes. Remove from oven and pour icing over cake while hot.

4. To prepare icing: Place cocoa, butter, and milk in a saucepan. Bring to a boil, stirring frequently. Remove from heat. Cool slightly. Add vanilla and powdered sugar. Mix until smooth. Use more milk if needed. Pour on cake.

Everything Cake

Donna Baxter

BAXTER'S STAINED GLASS

The batter looks a bit moist and runny for a cake, but it bakes beautifully. With no fat in the cake batter, you feel guilt-free about eating the rich icing.

Cake

- 2 eggs
- 2 cups sugar
- 1 teaspoon vanilla
- 2 cups flour
- 2 teaspoons baking soda
- 1 cup chopped nuts (pecans or english walnuts)
- 20 ounce can crushed pineapple (use juice)

Cream Cheese Frosting

- 8 ounces cream cheese
- 2 cups (scant) powdered sugar
- ½ cup margarine, softened
- 1 teaspoon vanilla

1. Preheat oven to 350°. Grease a 9" x 13" baking pan.

2. Mix everything together (cake ingredients only) in a large bowl. Pour batter into prepared pan. Bake for 40 to 45 minutes. Frost cake while still warm. Let stand at least 30 minutes before serving.

3. To prepare frosting: Mix everything together (frosting ingredients only). Spread on warm cake and sprinkle with additional nuts, if desired.

Jam Cake with Caramel Icing

Jane Malone

Jane received this dense old-fashioned cake from her Granny Wilcox. The cake itself is not too sweet. Iced with Granny Wilcox's Icing, it will satisfy all those with a serious sweet tooth. Part of Granny's recipe says to "fill hole in the middle with icing and give to Willie." Since Willie wasn't at my house, we served a "little of the middle" with each slice of cake.

Cake

- 1 cup butter or shortening
- 1 cup sugar
- 1 teaspoon baking soda
- 3 tablespoons buttermilk
- 1 cup applesauce
- 1 cup jam

- 1 teaspoon vanilla
- 3 large eggs
- 3 cups flour, sifted
- 1 cup raisins
- 1 cup black walnuts

Caramel Icing

- ½ cup butter
- 1 cup packed brown sugar

- ½ cup milk
- 2 cups powdered sugar, sifted

1. Preheat oven to 325°. Grease and flour a 10" tube pan.

2. Cream butter and sugar. Dissolve soda in buttermilk. Add to creamed mixture with applesauce, jam, vanilla, and eggs. Add flour, raisins, and black walnuts. Stir all ingredients together with a wooden spoon until blended. Do not use an electric mixer.

3. Pour into tube pan and bake for 50 to 60 minutes. Remove from pan. Ice cooled cake. Fill hole in middle with icing and "give to Willie."

4. To prepare icing: Melt butter in saucepan. Add brown sugar and milk. Bring to a boil. Boil for 1 minute stirring frequently. Remove from heat. Add powdered sugar. Beat with wooden spoon until smooth and thick. If too thick, add a little extra milk.

"Mississippi Mud Pie"

Vern Hippensteal
HIPPENSTEAL INN

This really is a cake, not a pie. It is the most popular dessert served at the Hippensteal Inn. I can just imagine sitting in a rocking chair on their balcony while looking out at the panoramic view of the Smokies. I bite into a slice of this rich chocolate treat, and slowly sip a hot cup of coffee. Life is good.

Cake

4 eggs, beaten	1 cup butter
2 cups sugar	⅓ cup cocoa
1 ½ cups flour	1 ½ cups chopped pecans
1 teaspoon vanilla	6 ½ ounces marshmallows

Fudge Frosting

½ cup butter, melted	16 ounces powdered sugar
⅓ cup milk	1 teaspoon vanilla
3 tablespoons cocoa	

1. Preheat oven to 350°. Grease a 9" x 13" pan.

2. In a large mixing bowl, combine eggs, sugar, flour, and vanilla. Melt butter in a saucepan and add cocoa. Add the egg mixture and beat well. Add the pecans. Pour into prepared pan and bake for 25 to 30 minutes.

3. As soon as the cake is removed from the oven, cover it with marshmallows. Return the pan to the oven until marshmallows are slightly melted. Pour on frosting.

4. To make frosting: Combine butter, milk, and cocoa. Beat in the powdered sugar and vanilla. Pour the frosting over the marshmallows and cool before cutting into pieces.

Pig Picking Cake

Margaret Seymour
SEYMOUR'S COUNTRY CRAFTS

This cake looks sensational, tastes fantastic, and is almost too simple to be true. It is one of my favorite recipes in this book.

Cake

1 box yellow cake mix
½ cup oil
4 eggs

11 ounce can mandarin oranges (use juice)

Pineapple Whip Frosting

3 ounce package instant vanilla pudding

9 ounce container frozen whipped topping, defrosted
1 large can pineapple (use juice)

1. Preheat oven to 325°. Grease four 8" round cake pans.

2. In a large bowl, beat cake mix, oil, eggs, and mandarin oranges. Divide batter evenly in the 4 pans and bake for 15 minutes. Remove from pan. When cake is completely cool, spread frosting on top of each layer. Frost sides and top of cake. Refrigerate before serving.

3. To prepare frosting: blend together vanilla pudding mix, whipped topping, and pineapple. Spread frosting on cooled cake.

Stack Cake

Kathy Shields Guttman

Gena Lewis gave me a method for making Stack Cake: Make four plate-size sugar cookies and spread with jam or applesauce between the layers. She suggested cooking dried apples, along with cinnamon, sugar, and applesauce for a filling. Since I did not have an actual recipe to follow, I created my own. If I do say so myself, it is quite good. It reminds me of a giant Fig Newton cookie.

1 tablespoon butter
3 apples, peeled, cored, and chopped
¼ cup apple juice
⅓ cup brown sugar
½ teaspoon cinnamon
¼ teaspoon nutmeg
3 cups dried apples, pre-soaked and drained
¼ cup molasses
sugar cookie stacks

1. In a heavy skillet, melt butter and add apples. Saute for 5 minutes on medium heat. Stir frequently. Add apple juice, brown sugar, cinnamon, nutmeg, and dried apples. Simmer on medium low heat for 15 minutes, stirring frequently. Add molasses and continue to cook for another 15 minutes, stirring frequently. Mixture should be thick.

2. While mixture is warm, spread between layers, starting and ending with a cookie stack. The cookies will soften once spread with warm mixture.

3. Cookie stacks: Make four 8" round cookies using your favorite sugar cookie recipe. I used Donna Baxter's **Sugar Cookies** recipe in this book. It makes four 8" stacks with enough dough leftover for 3 dozen cookies. You may bake cookie stacks 1 or 2 days before making cake.

Sunshine Cake

Gena Lewis
LEWIS FAMILY CRAFTS

This treasured family recipe came from Gena's mother-in-law, Helen Cooke. Gena says, "She was an old-fashioned cook. I loved her dearly. She was a great lady, and knew how to bake great pies and cakes. She's been gone 12 years and I still miss her. She taught me a lot." Quite a testament to a special mother-in-law.

This cake takes a little more care to produce, but it is definitely worth the effort. Try serving it with a scoop of ice cream and some fresh strawberries.

6 eggs, separated
1 teaspoon cream of tartar
1 ½ cups sugar
½ cup water

1 cup cake flour, sifted 4 times
1 teaspoon vanilla
1 teaspoon almond extract

1. In a large bowl beat egg whites until frothy. Add cream of tartar and beat until stiff.

2. In a small sauce pan, boil sugar and water together until it spins a thread (about 225 to 230° on a candy thermometer) when tested in cold water. Beat this mixture into egg whites and continue to beat until almost cool.

3. Preheat oven to 325°. Beat egg yolks in a separate bowl. Add to egg whites. Fold in sifted flour. Add vanilla and almond extract and fold gently.

4. Pour into large ungreased angel food pan and bake for 1 hour. Invert pan on wire rack and cool before removing from pan.

Lewis Family Crafts

Mike Lewis spends the days at his workshop making unusual and practical wood products: Everything from magic folding baskets, banana stands, and baseball cap displays; to oak clocks and shelves, wine racks, and bread boxes. His wife, Gena, displays and sells their crafts from their studio in the Morning Mist complex. On weekends in late summer, they sell their crafts at a Renaissance Fair in Ohio.

When not working in their studio, Gena enjoys spending time on her hobbies: historical research, genealogy, and collecting old cookbooks. In her limited spare time, she is writing a cookbook combining her interests. In this labor of love she is incorporating family history, along with recipes, from three to four generations of families connected to her.

These two crafters have a strong sense of family. Gena says, "In our family, fun is associated with meals; we love to cook and eat." And they know about good food; both how to cook it, and where to find it. They know wonderful out-of-the-way restaurants with great food. And, after trying the many delicious recipes Gena has contributed to this book, I think you will agree that, like the crafts they make, some are unusual and some practical, but all are good. Do try her **Vanilla Wafer Cake**, it is one of my favorites. Her mother-in-law's **Sunshine Cake** is one of Gena's treasured recipes.

Vanilla Wafer Cake

Gena Lewis
LEWIS FAMILY CRAFTS

Gena acquired this recipe from her new daughter-in-law's family down in Louisiana. Gena says "it only takes a small piece, but you will want more—it is scrumptious!"

1 cup margarine
2 cups sugar
6 eggs (may use equivalent amount
    of substitute)
1 teaspoon vanilla

½ cup milk
4 cups crushed vanilla wafers
7 ounces flaked coconut
1 cup chopped nuts

1. Preheat oven to 350°. Grease and flour 10-cup tube pan.

2. In a large bowl, cream margarine until fluffy. While beating, gradually add sugar until light and fluffy. Add eggs and beat well. Add vanilla, milk, vanilla wafers, coconut, and nuts. Fold in until well mixed. Do not overbeat.

3. Pour into prepared cake pan and bake for 1 hour and 25 minutes.

Variation: You can delete the nuts and bake in 2 loaf pans (adjust cooking time down) and call it **Coconut Bread**.

Quilts by Wilma

Wilma Prebor's first quilt shop in Gatlinburg was so small, she had nightmares about it. She dreamt the showcase was in front of the door and everything behind her so tightly packed that she had to stand at the door while customers would point and say "I want one of this and one of that." It was just too crowded for them to get inside.

She now has a large, lovely gallery in what used to be a church. Exquisite handstitched quilts hang from the high ceiling. The rest of her extensive inventory is displayed on several round racks. She also carries quilting supplies and pre-cut kits; fabric; embroidery kits and supplies; a colorful array of silk ribbon; and books and videos to motivate and teach you.

Wilma says there would not have been a shop like this if it were not for "Grandma's quilt"; a wool quilt made from hand-woven fabric from garments her great grandparents brought with them from Germany. It started her on quilting as a hobby. When she found herself in a position where she had to support herself, she felt fortunate to take something she loved doing and make a living out of it. She opened her first quilt shop over 25 years ago.

Wilma loves expressing her creativity in cooking as well as crafts. Baking and cake decorating are a specialty of hers. Next time you bake a cake, top it with **Wilma's Favorite Icing**.

Wilma's Favorite Icing

Wilma Prebor
QUILTS BY WILMA

Wilma says this is a great icing for any kind of cake. She has used this on everything from Red Devils Food Cake to wedding cakes. She got this recipe while still living at home. It was the only icing liked by her father. Its texture is a cross between whipped cream and marshmallow, yet it is not too sweet. The recipe makes enough to cover an 8" or 9" square cake, or the top of a 9" x 13" cake. It may be doubled for larger cakes. Try it on your favorite cake.

2 ½ tablespoons flour	¼ cup butter
½ cup milk	½ cup sugar
¼ cup shortening	¼ teaspoon salt

1. In a small saucepan, blend flour and milk with a whisk. Cook over medium heat to a thick paste, stirring constantly. Cool to lukewarm.

2. In a mixing bowl, cream together shortening, butter, sugar, and salt. When paste is cool enough to put your finger in (Should be just warm like "baby's milk." If paste is too cool, it leaves lumps in icing; if too warm, it melts the creamed mixture.), beat into butter mixture with electric mixer until fluffy. Ice cake.

Green Apple Pie

Kathy Shields Guttman

This is an old family recipe handed down to me from my mother, Ruth Simmons Shields, passed down to her from my grandmother, Ida Josephine Walker Simmons, passed to her by my great grandmother Dora Josephine Hatcher Walker of Louisville, Kentucky. When the grandmothers were making pies they used lard, shortening was not available.

Leftover pie dough may be used for **Roly-Polys**. My mother offers this advice with her recipe "Once the pie is done, cool on a rack and hide the serving spatula until dinner. Forget the calories and enjoy...you can diet tomorrow."

Dough for crust

3 cups flour	1 cup and 3 tablespoons vegetable
⅛ to ¼ teaspoon salt	shortening
	8 ounce glass ice cold water

Apple filling

6 or 7 large Granny Smith apples	cinnamon
¾ to 1 cup sugar	nutmeg
2 tablespoons flour	2 teaspoons butter or margarine
salt	milk and sugar

1. Before dough: Peel, core, and slice apples. Place in large bowl with enough water to cover fruit. Fill 8-ounce glass with ice cubes, add water, and set aside for crust.

2. To prepare dough: In a large bowl, combine flour and salt. Cut in shortening (pea-size pieces). Add ice water (start with 3 or 4 tablespoons, use as much as necessary as long as its cold). Work gently through flour with forks to form dough, do not overwork.

3. Place a little more than half the dough on a well-floured board. Roll dough in flour, form into a ball, then gently flatten. Roll dough to fit a 9" pie pan. Cut away excess dough. Roll top crust and set aside.

4. To prepare apple filling: Drain apples. Arrange half the slices in crust. Combine sugar and flour. Sprinkle half of sugar mixture on apples. Sprinkle with liberal amount of

cinnamon, and dash of nutmeg. Add remaining apples, rest of sugar, and sprinkle with cinnamon and another dash of nutmeg. Cut margarine into bits and arrange over surface. Brush ice water on outer edges of bottom crust. Place top crust over apples. Seal edges of top and bottom together, fluting with your thumb. Cut away excess dough.

5. In center of top crust, slice a couple of lines, about 2 inches long, to allow steam to escape. Brush top crust with small amount of milk and sprinkle with sugar. Preheat oven to 350°. Bake for 50 to 60 minutes.

Roly-Polys

Kathy Shields Guttman

Roly-polys are like a rich cinnamon roll. They are a companion dessert to my mother's **Green Apple Pie**. They were a must at our house. My mother always planned on having enough extra dough to make them.

leftover pie dough	cinnamon
sugar	milk and sugar
butter or margarine	

1. Roll dough into a very thin sheet. Sprinkle liberally with sugar. Dot evenly (every 1 or 2 inches) with small dots of butter. Sprinkle generously with cinnamon. Start rolling at the long edge and continue to roll as tightly as possible.

2. Pick up the roll and curve into a half moon shape to fit in a pie tin. Brush lightly with milk and sprinkle with sugar. Bake at the same time and temperature as the pie. If the roll is quite thick, it may take a bit longer for it to bake. Bake until nicely browned and a little of the inside syrup begins to ooze out. Let cool for 10 minutes before cutting into slices. Prepare to referee as to who gets the last slice.

Angel Pie

Betty Jane Posey
BETTY JANE POSEY GALLERY

One bite of this heavenly delight and you will be shouting "Hallelujah." It looks and tastes extraordinary, yet it is easy and quick to prepare. To save calories, eliminate the whipped cream and substitute a frozen whipped topping.

3 egg whites
1 teaspoon vanilla
1 cup sugar
1 cup graham cracker crumbs
1 cup chopped pecans

1 teaspoon baking powder
½ cup whipping cream or frozen
   whipped topping
Maraschino cherries, optional

1. Grease and flour a 9" pie plate. Preheat oven to 325°. Beat egg whites and vanilla until soft peaks form. Gradually add sugar, beating until stiff.

2. Combine cracker crumbs, pecans, and baking powder and fold into meringue mixture. Spread evenly in prepared pie plate. Bake for 20 to 25 minutes. Cool completely.

3. Whip the cream until stiff. Cut pie in wedges and top with a dollop of whipped cream and a maraschino cherry.

"I paint almost all the time, whether on canvas, on paper, or in my own thoughts. As long as I am able to paint, as long as the delight, excitement, and creativity is there, I will continue to make my original paintings available to the collectors who have supported my work for so many years."

—Betty Jane Posey
Betty Jane Posey Gallery

Japanese Fruit Pie

Sue Ownby
E & T Woodcarvings

Sue says this is a very good, very rich recipe handed down to her from her grand-mother, Vera Clubine Maples Robinson. Thanks Sue for sharing this recipe. It is truly unique and delicious, as well as being easy to prepare.

2 eggs	½ cup chopped dates
1 cup sugar	½ cup coconut
½ cup margarine, softened	½ cup pecans, coarsely chopped
1 teaspoon vanilla	9" unbaked pie shell

1. Preheat oven to 400°. Beat eggs until lemon colored. Add sugar, margarine, vanilla, dates, coconut, and pecans. Beat together until well blended.

2. Pour mixture into pie shell. Bake at 400° for 10 minutes and then reduce temperature to 350°. Bake for another 20 minutes until crust is golden brown.

Lemon juice removes rust and mildew in old quilts and other materials.

—Sue Ownby
E & T Woodcarvings

Gemstone

*Y*ou can't tell a book by its cover," is the first thought that comes to mind when you walk into Mac and Susan McDonell's Studio. Not much in the way of fancy decor, but when you peer into the glass display cases, you find beautifully designed custom jewelry. A fine selection of sparkling gemstones and Tennessee freshwater pearls are set in 14 K gold and sterling silver in both unique as well as traditional styles. Colorful slices of crystal geodes are showcased amongst the jewels.

Two of the most valuable gems in this studio are the artisans themselves. Charter members of the Great Smoky Arts & Crafts Community for well over 20 years, they combine their lives and talents. Mac casts and sets jewelry, is a story teller extraordinare, and cooks up a storm. Susan designs and repairs jewelry, runs the business, and is a great "straightman" for Mac's stories.

Not much for following recipes, Mac creates dishes as he goes along. He instinctively knows presentation is important. His simple appetizer, **Shrimp and Cheese Gem**, makes a magnificent centerpiece for a buffet; and his **Key Lime Pie** topped with green candy sprinkles and a maraschino cherry looks as good as it tastes. His recipes, along with his stories, are always served with a dash of style.

Key Lime Pie

Mac McDonell
GEMSTONE

"At a restaurant in the late 1930s down in the Keys, this recipe was more secret than anything in this world." Mac says, "Nobody, under the threat of death, would give it out." He had a girlfriend working there. He tried to con it out of her, but even after a year he still could not get it. Finally she said, "Well, I'll give it to you, but if you tell anybody, so help me I'll shoot you, because they're going to shoot me if they find out!" Mac could not believe what she told him. "The recipe is so simple, it hurts," he says, "and I still haven't tasted anything better."

The secret Mac learned is quite clever: pile meringue as high as you can and then use a blowtorch to brown it. If you do not want to make a meringue, or if you do not have a torch handy, just top it with whipped cream.

Key lime pie

14 ounce can sweetened condensed milk
3 egg yolks
½ cup fresh key lime juice

9" graham cracker crust
green sprinkles and maraschino cherry, optional
whipped cream, optional

Meringue

3 egg whites
¼ teaspoon cream of tartar

¼ cup sugar

1. Place condensed milk in a mixing bowl. Gently stir in egg yolks. Gently stir in lime juice (the lime juice "cooks" the eggs). Do not whip, just stir it until it thickens. Pour into graham crust.

2. Spread meringue on top, sealing edges. Brown with a blow torch. Or, you may brown by placing it in a 400 degree oven for 8 minutes until brown. Chill before serving. Place green sprinkles and maraschino cherry on top. You may skip the meringue and just top with whipped cream.

3. To prepare meringue: Beat egg whites with an electric mixer until peaks begin to form. Add ¼ teaspoon cream of tartar and continue beating. Gradually add ¼ cup sugar and continue to beat until shiny stiff peaks form.

Lemon Meringue Pie

Wilma Prebor
Quilts by Wilma

Wilma loved her Grandma's lemon pie. But when Grandma came to visit, Wilma had time only to make Jell-O Lemon Pie. When Grandma tasted it and found out how easy it was, she declared she was born 50 years too soon. Next time Wilma visited Grandma, she had lemon pie filling in her cupboard. Wilma now makes her pie from scratch just like Grandma.

Lemon pie filling

1 ⅛ cups sugar	2 tablespoons butter
¼ cup cornstarch	3 tablespoons lemon juice
1 ⅛ cups water	1 tablespoon grated lemon rind
2 egg yolks, beaten	8" baked pie shell

Meringue

2 egg whites	¼ cup sugar
¼ teaspoon cream of tartar	

1. To prepare lemon filling: In a medium saucepan combine sugar and cornstarch. Slowly stir in water. Cook over medium heat, stirring constantly until mixture is smooth and comes to a boil. Boil 1 minute then remove from heat and slowly stir in half the hot mixture into beaten yolks. Pour yolk mixture back into saucepan and bring back to a boil for 1 minute, stirring constantly.

2. Remove from heat and blend in butter, lemon juice, and lemon rind. Pour into pie shell. While mixture is still hot, top with meringue being sure to seal it to the edges of the crust. Bake in pre-heated oven at 400° for about 8 minutes until brown.

3. To prepare meringue: In medium mixing bowl, beat egg whites with cream of tartar until frothy. Gradually beat in sugar until dissolved and meringue forms stiff peaks.

Variation: When you do not wish to heat up your oven, use a commercial graham cracker crust and top lemon filling with a whipped topping.

Old-Fashioned Chess Pie

Betty Jane Posey
BETTY JANE POSEY GALLERY

This standard southern favorite, is very much like an old-fashioned Quebec Sugar Pie. The recipe may be divided in half for one pie.

2 cups sugar
1 teaspoon flour
1 cup butter, softened
2 whole eggs

4 egg yolks
1 teaspoon vanilla
two 8" unbaked pie shells

1. In a large mixing bowl, combine sugar and flour. Add softened butter and cream together thoroughly until the consistency of whipped cream. Add unbeaten eggs, and egg yolks, one at a time. Add vanilla.

2. Preheat oven to 450°. Divide filling into pie shells. Bake for 10 minutes, then reduce heat to 350° for 30 minutes.

Pecan Pie

Eleanor Hopf
SCHUCKS Y'ALL

After just one bite, your guests will be saying "Schucks Y'all, this is good pie!" Eleanor's version of this easy dessert makes two pies, one of which may be frozen for future use.

2 cups pecans, divided
2 unbaked pie shells
1 cup margarine, melted
1 cup dark corn syrup

1 cup sugar
1 teaspoon vanilla
3 eggs

1. Preheat oven to 350°. Place 1 cup of the pecan halves in each pie shell. In medium bowl, mix cooled margarine with corn syrup, sugar, and vanilla on low speed of mixer. Slowly beat in eggs.

2. Pour mixture on top of pecans in pie shell. Bake in oven for 45 to 55 minutes until lightly brown.

Blender Pecan Pie

Wilma Prebor
QUILTS BY WILMA

People go nuts over homemade pecan pie. When you serve it, they are impressed with your culinary skills. These are people that have never attempted baking a pecan pie.

This is one of the easiest and quickest recipes you will ever make. Use a store-bought frozen pie shell, mix your ingredients together, bake and prepare for compliments!

2 eggs	2 tablespoons butter, melted
⅔ cup sugar	1 teaspoon vanilla
½ teaspoon salt	1 cup pecans, plus extra
½ cup light corn syrup	9" unbaked pie shell

1. Preheat oven to 425°. In a blender, or food processor, place eggs, sugar, salt, corn syrup, butter, and vanilla. Blend well. Add 1 cup pecans and blend just enough to coarsely chop nuts.

2. Pour mixture into pie shell. Place extra pecan halves on top. Bake at 425° for 15 minutes. Reduce heat to 350° and bake for another 30 minutes until lightly browned.

Dorothy's Incredible Pie

Martha Powers
OSTEEN & POWERS

I never did understand the saying 'It's as easy as Pie'. Making a pie is not easy. For years I've struggled with pie crusts. Rest assured, this recipe really is easy. It makes its own crust with a creamy filling inside and a crisp topping of coconut on top.

½ cup self-rising flour
1 ⅓ cups sugar
4 eggs, beaten
2 cups milk

¼ cup margarine, softened
1 teaspoon vanilla
7 ounces coconut, canned or
    packaged

1. Preheat oven to 375°. Lightly grease a 9" deep dish pie plate or casserole dish.

2. In a large bowl, combine flour and sugar. Add eggs, milk, margarine, and vanilla. Beat until thoroughly mixed and then stir in coconut.

3. Pour into pie plate or round casserole and bake for 30 to 40 minutes.

Helen's Cornshuck Crafts

*H*elen Vance's little studio is alive with colorful flowers, wreaths, and arrangements made from cornshucks. She uses a rainbow of different colors to make her cornshuck creations. Beautiful as well as practical, all you need to do is "blow off the dust" to maintain them. Also displayed in her studio are miniature cornshuck dolls and various old-fashioned wooden toys of the type young Appalachian children played with many years ago.

A Gatlinburg native, Helen's family has a long history and future in crafts. Her mother wove chair bottoms. Helen opened her own studio after working at the Arrowmont School of Arts and Crafts for 17 years. Her husband records the images of the Smokies with photography, and her daughter does stained glass, along with working in other art forms.

Helen does not have much time to cook these days, but every now and then she enjoys baking a pumpkin pie just like her Mom used to make.

Pumpkin Pie

Helen Vance
Helen's Cornshuck Crafts

Pumpkin pie is one of my all time favorites. Helen's recipe, handed down from her mother, Flora Reagan, has an interesting twist with its crystallized sugar top. This pie would be a welcome addition at your next holiday meal, but why wait that long. Make one up soon and take it with you on a picnic, or just sit in a cozy chair and enjoy a slice.

2 eggs	2 tablespoons melted butter
¾ cup sugar	¼ cup evaporated milk
½ teaspoon cinnamon	1 cup pumpkin
¼ teaspoon nutmeg	8" unbaked pie shell
1 teaspoon vanilla	additional 2 teaspoons sugar

1. Preheat oven to 350°. In a large bowl, beat eggs. Add sugar, cinnamon, nutmeg, vanilla, butter, and evaporated milk. Mix well. Add pumpkin. Beat until smooth.

2. Pour into pie shell. Bake for 25 minutes. Remove briefly from oven and sprinkle with additional sugar over the top and return to oven. Bake for another 20 minutes. The sugar will give the pie a crystallized top.

Note: If you use canned pumpkin to prepare this recipe, try using the leftover pumpkin by making up a batch of **Pumpkin Cranberry Muffins**.

Otto Preske—Artist in Wood

O tto Preske still has his first carving—a neckerchief slide, made while he was a Boy Scout. While working as a commercial artist, he met a wood carver from Portugal who showed him how to use professional wood carving tools. Carving on and off since the age of 12, Otto wanted to make a career of it, so he and his family moved to Gatlinburg and opened their own shop for the 1976 season.

Otto enjoys meeting people from all over the world in his shop. His wood carvings and sculptures are in churches and homes across the United States, Europe, and even Australia.

When you enter his shop, there is a bulletin board with thank you notes and pictures of his carvings and wood sculptures in the homes and places of their proud and pleased owners.

Otto is still involved in the Scouts. He has been a leader for over 15 years. Currently he is assistant District Commissioner and, as a Deacon, the Chaplain for Scouting in the Catholic Diocese of Knoxville.

Picnicing in the Chimneys picnic area, and chasing away the bears from their food, is a favorite activity of the Preske family. Otto's recipe for **Wood Chip Pie** would be a welcome treat for any picnic.

Wood Chip Pie

Otto Preske
Otto Preske—Artist in Wood

Who else but a wood carver would contribute this wonderful recipe for Wood Chip Pie. My family whittled away this delicious dessert in record time. The recipe makes enough filling for a scant 10" pie or a 9" pie with enough extra filling for a couple of small tarts—the cook's sneak treat!

2 cups sugar
2 tablespoons cornmeal
4 eggs
¼ cup melted butter

¼ cup lemon juice
¼ cup milk
½ to ¾ cups sliced almonds
Unbaked pie crust

1. Preheat oven to 375°. In a mixing bowl, beat sugar, cornmeal, and eggs until well blended. While still beating, add melted butter, lemon juice, and milk. Stir in sliced almonds and then pour into an unbaked pie crust.

2. Bake for 35 to 40 minutes or until nice and brown on top. If you wish, you may sprinkle additional sliced almonds on top after baking.

"Talent is a gift from God. What we do with it is our gift to him."

Otto Preske
Otto Preske—Artist in Wood

E & T Woodcarvings

Eugene Ownby has been carving for over 30 years. He magically transforms a humble hunk of wood into everything from simply carved hummingbirds and mountain men to delicately detailed and handpainted grey wolves, bears, and passenger pigeons.

Like so many other families with their roots in Gatlinburg, Eugene and Sue's craft abilities and creativity seem to be part of their genetic make-up. Eugene's parents were craftspeople. They made chairs and bark baskets. Sue's mother and step-father wove nylon handbags and placemats. Their weaving shop belonged to the craft community when it first started.

Eugene is training the next generation. His sons Jeff and Tony, are also practicing the art of carving. His eyes brighten as he talks about how both are good carvers and, just like he did, will become even better in time.

While Eugene works at his carving, his wife Sue has her own specialties. Not only does she help at the shop and paint some of Eugene's finished carvings, she is also well known for her craft of cooking. Her **Fried Apple Pies** are legendary. Don't miss trying Sue's recipes, she truly has a knack for good cooking.

Fried Apple Pies

Sue Ownby
E & T Woodcarvings

A signature recipe for this book, you must try Sue's pies. They take a little time and work, but they are worth it. These are beautifully crisp and brown on the outside, and steaming hot and moist on the inside with a buttery apple filling. They may be frozen and reheated in an oven or microwave (the oven works best).

Filling

4 large apples, peeled, cored, and sliced	¼ cup butter
	½ cup sugar

Dough

2 cups self-rising flour	½ to ⅔ cup milk
2 tablespoons vegetable shortening	vegetable oil or shortening for frying

1. In a large iron skillet, fry apples on medium high heat with butter and sugar. Cook, stirring occasionally, until liquid evaporates to a syrup-like (apples take on a translucent appearance) consistency, takes about 15 minutes. Watch carefully, stirring frequently, until liquid is completely absorbed, takes about another 10 minutes. Be careful not to burn apples. Remove from heat. Cool and refrigerate. Mixture may be prepared 2 days in advance.

2. Prepare dough and divide into 1 ½" balls. Roll each ball to the size of a saucer. Put a spoonful of cold apples on one side. Fold the other half over the apples. Press the sides together with your finger, or a fork.

3. In a large iron skillet, heat vegetable shortening or oil until hot (about ⅓" to ½" deep). Drop pies into hot oil and cook until brown. Flip over and brown the other side. Cool on paper towel.

4. To prepare dough: Cut flour and shortening together. Add enough milk to make a stiff dough. Makes about 20 pies.

Note: You may use dried apple slices, that have been reconstituted, instead of fresh. This recipe may be doubled for more pies.

Baked Fried Apple Pies

Joan McGill

GLADES DELI

While making the eight-mile loop around the craft community to collect recipes and anecdotes for this book, I became addicted to Joan's fried apple pies. Some days I was lucky enough to be there just as they came out of the oven.

Apple Filling

3 tablespoons butter	1 teaspoon cinnamon
3 large apples, peeled and sliced	1 tablespoon flour
⅓ cup sugar	

Dough

2 ½ cups self-rising flour	⅔ to ¾ cup buttermilk
¾ cup shortening	extra sugar

1. To prepare filling: Melt butter in large skillet. Add apples, sugar, cinnamon, and flour. Cook on medium heat, stirring occasionally, until liquid evaporates to a syrup consistency. Takes about 12 minutes. Continue stirring frequently until liquid is absorbed, another 8 to 10 minutes. Do not burn apples. Remove from heat and cool. May be prepared 2 days in advance.

2. To make turnovers: Preheat oven to 375°. Lightly grease a baking sheet. Place a dollop of apple filling on the dough. Fold dough over filling, sealing edges with thumb, then with a fork. Place on baking sheet. Sprinkle with sugar. Bake 18 to 22 minutes until lightly browned. Remove and cool on racks. Makes 8 to 10.

3. To prepare dough: In a large mixing bowl, combine self-rising flour and shortening. Cut into coarse crumbs. Blend in enough milk with a fork until dough leaves sides of bowl. Knead gently on floured surface 10 to 14 strokes. Pinch off dough balls 2" to 2 ½" wide. Roll each one, on a floured surface, into an oval about 6" x 7".

COOKIES,
CANDIES & SQUARES

Frosted Chocolate Drop Cookies

Kathy Shields Guttman

This is my mother's recipe. She considers them a special occasion treat due to the lengthy preparation time. She melts the chocolate and butter in a double boiler, heats the milk in a saucepan, and beats the ingredients with a mixer. Then she cleans everything by hand.

Well Mom, try the "techno way." Use a microwave to melt the chocolate and butter and heat milk. Use a food processor to cream shortening and sugar. Pulse in dry ingredients for cookies, and beat ingredients for icing. Put mess in the dishwasher, while you sit on the porch and enjoy a coffee.

Cookies

¼ cup vegetable shortening	1 teaspoon vanilla
1 cup light brown sugar	1 ½ cups flour
1 egg, well beaten	½ teaspoon baking soda
½ cup milk	1 cup chopped nuts
2 squares melted chocolate	

Chocolate Drop Frosting

2 tablespoons butter	3 tablespoons hot milk
2 ounces semi-sweet chocolate	½ teaspoon vanilla
1 ½ cups sifted powdered sugar	dash salt

1. Cream shortening and brown sugar until fluffy. Add egg and mix well. Add small amount of milk and melted chocolate. Add vanilla and whip until well blended.

2. Alternately add flour, mixed with baking soda, and remaining milk. Mix well. Mix in nuts, a few at a time, with each addition of flour and milk.

3. Place batter in refrigerator to chill for at least 20 minutes. Preheat oven to 350°. Grease cookie sheets. Drop chilled batter from a spoon onto cookie sheet. Bake for 10 to 12 minutes. Test with toothpick. Do not bake too dry. Frost when cool. Makes 3 dozen.

4. To make frosting: Melt butter and chocolate together. Stir until blended. Place powdered sugar into mixing bowl. Add hot milk, beating until smooth. Stir in vanilla, salt, and chocolate mixture. Beat until smooth and thickened, about 5 minutes.

Ginger Snap Cookies

Joan McGill
Glades Deli

Joan says these cookies improve with age, and she's right. The only problem is finding a hiding spot. The wonderful aroma wafting through the house is a dead giveaway you are baking some old-fashioned, "just like grandma used to make," cookies. It may be wise to offer your family one or two cookies each before hiding, making them promise not to hunt down the cookie tin for at least a week.

¾ cup shortening
1 cup sugar
¼ cup molasses
1 egg, or 2 egg whites, well beaten
2 cups flour

2 teaspoons baking soda
1 teaspoon cinnamon
1 teaspoon ginger
1 teaspoon ground cloves
additional 3 tablespoons sugar

1. Preheat oven to 350°. Lightly grease cookie sheet.

2. Cream together thoroughly shortening and 1 cup sugar. Add molasses and egg. Mix well. Sift together flour, baking soda, cinnamon, ginger, and cloves. Add to creamed mixture. Beat until smooth. Batter will be quite stiff.

3. Shape dough into walnut-sized balls. Roll in additional sugar. Place 2" apart on cookie sheet. Bake for 12 to 15 minutes until cookie edges are browned. Cool on racks. Store cooled cookies in airtight container.

Note: Being the cinnamon fan that I am, when it came time to rolling cookie dough balls into sugar, I rolled half the cookies in plain sugar and then added some cinnamon to the sugar to roll the rest.

Old Favorite Oatmeal Cookies

Wilma Prebor
QUILTS BY WILMA

Money was scarce when Wilma was first married. Out of necessity, she learned how to make ends meet. Her neighbor would save the fat for her whenever she cooked bacon. One day having a craving for oatmeal cookies, but no shortening to make them with, she used bacon fat. Wilma refers to these as her "Old Favorites" and prefers, to this day, to make her oatmeal cookies with bacon fat.

If you wish, you may replace any amount of the bacon fat with vegetable shortening.

1 cup bacon fat	1 teaspoon baking soda
1 cup sugar	1 teaspoon cinnamon
2 eggs, beaten	¼ teaspoon salt
¼ cup milk	2 cups oatmeal (not instant)
2 cups flour	1 cup raisins, or nuts

1. Cream together bacon fat and sugar. Beat in eggs and milk. Sift together flour, baking soda, cinnamon, and salt. Mix into batter. Stir in oatmeal and raisins.

2. Preheat oven to 375°. Lightly grease cookie pan. Using a spoon, drop batter onto cookie sheet. Place 2" apart. Bake for 12 to 15 minutes until brown. Makes about 3 dozen cookies.

Old English Tea Cakes

Buie Boling
Buie Pottery

This is Buie's grandmother's (Margaret McConnaughey) favorite cookie. Buie says they are worth the effort to make, but be warned, there may be a fight over who gets the last one.

Buie's Mom complained she was giving away the best family secret with this recipe. Subconsciously I think Buie believed her. When she first sent me this recipe she left out one "minor" ingredient, the flour.

½ cup butter or margarine
1 cup sugar
1 egg
vanilla and/or nutmeg to taste

2 cups flour
½ teaspoon baking soda
½ teaspoon cream of tartar
pinch of salt

1. Thoroughly cream together butter and sugar. Beat in egg and vanilla. Sift together flour, baking soda, cream of tartar, and salt. Mix into creamed mixture. Chill dough (several hours in refrigerator or 1 hour in freezer).

2. Preheat oven to 375°. Roll out (the thinner the better) dough on floured board. Cut with cookie cutters and place on ungreased cookie sheet. Bake for 10 to 12 minutes. Watch carefully, do not burn.

"Being an artist in a tourist town is a lot of fun, but very trying at times; such as being cheerful and friendly (and mean it!) to the 5 zillion people that come through your door. Or, being asked as I sit at my potters' wheel, splattered all over in mud, 'So, do you make this stuff here?' Sigh..."

Buie Boling
Buie Pottery

Peanut Butter Cookies

Joan Royer
Bunnies n Bears by Joan

Joan's cookies will put a smile on the face of your family and friends and even "Bunnies n Bears." Try rolling some of the dough balls in a mixture of cinnamon, sugar, and nutmeg before baking for a slightly spicy version.

¼ cup shortening
¼ cup butter
½ cup peanut butter
½ cup white sugar
½ cup brown sugar

1 egg, beaten
1 ¼ cups flour
½ teaspoon baking powder
¼ teaspoon baking soda
¼ teaspoon salt

1. Cream together shortening, butter, and peanut butter. Beat in white sugar and brown sugar. Mix in egg. Sift together flour, baking powder, baking soda, and salt. Stir into creamed mixture. Chill dough.

2. Preheat oven to 375°. Roll chilled dough into walnut-sized balls. Place 3" apart on lightly greased baking sheet. Flatten with fork dipped in flour, crisscross style. Bake for 10 to 12 minutes at 375°. Bake until set, but not hard. Cool on rack. Makes 3 dozen.

Scotch Shortbread

Gena Lewis
LEWIS FAMILY CRAFTS

Gena forgets where this recipe came from, but her friend Edith, originally from Scotland, gave some to her Dad. He said it couldn't be as good as his shortbread, but he loved it.

1 cup margarine, softened	**2 cups flour**
½ cup powdered sugar	**¼ teaspoon salt**

1. Preheat oven to 300°. Lightly grease a 9" x 9" pan.

2. Cream together margarine and powdered sugar. Add flour and salt and mix into a stiff dough.

3. Press dough into pan. Prick top with a fork and bake for 25 to 35 minutes until a light golden color. Remove from oven, cool slightly and slice.

"My cooking experience has been widely varied. I grew up with southern cooking, married into a part German family and learned German cooking. I lived in a Greek/Italian neighborhood for 11 years and learned how to enjoy the food of these two countries. Then I lived two years in El Paso, Texas and learned what real Mexican food tasted like. I also acquired Scottish dishes from a Scottish friend."

—Gena Lewis
Lewis Family Crafts

Mountain Scotch Shortbread

Betty Jane Posey
Betty Jane Posey Gallery

Scotch Shortbread is a mountain favorite. Betty Jane's version is just a little sweeter than Gena's. Try them both, then experiment with your own. I like to make a mixture of granulated sugar, cinnamon, and chopped bittersweet chocolate and press the cookie dough into the mixture before baking.

1 cup butter, softened
½ cup powdered sugar
2 cups flour

⅛ teaspoon salt
¼ teaspoon baking powder
powdered sugar

1. Preheat oven to 325°. Cream butter and sugar until light. Add sifted flour, salt, and baking powder. Mix into a dough.

2. Roll dough ½" thick on wax paper. Sprinkle with powdered sugar. Cut into shapes or squares. Place on ungreased cookie sheet. Bake for 15 minutes until light brown. While hot, sprinkle with additional powdered sugar.

Swiss Mocha Hazelnut Cookies

Kathy Shields Guttman

Being in a creative mood one afternoon, I concocted this combination of my favorite flavors, chocolate, coffee, and hazelnuts, into a shortbread cookie.

Dough

½ cup butter, softened
⅓ cup sugar
½ cup toasted hazelnuts, ground
1 cup flour
¼ teaspoon cinnamon

1 ounce semi-sweet chocolate, grated
1 tablespoon Swiss mocha instant coffee powder
2 tablespoons hot water

Topping

½ ounce semi-sweet chocolate, grated

2 teaspoons sugar
⅛ teaspoon cinnamon

1. Cream butter and sugar. Combine hazelnuts, flour, cinnamon, and chocolate. Mix with creamed butter. Dissolve coffee in hot water. Add to batter. Mix ingredients until well combined, kneading with your hands if necessary. Pinch off a teaspoon of batter and form into a ball.

2. Preheat oven to 325°. Press dough balls into topping mixture and flatten into a round on an ungreased cookie sheet. Bake for 15 to 17 minutes. Makes 2 dozen.

3. To make topping: In a small bowl, combine grated chocolate, sugar, and cinnamon.

Note: Hazelnuts may be toasted in a microwave, on high, for 1 to 1 ½ minutes.

Baxter's Stained Glass

*T*he large windows running the length of this studio, make the perfect backdrop to display colorful stained glass suncatchers, hanging window panels, lamp shades, and more. Glass shelves showcase their popular three-dimensional angels, candle holders, stars, and alphabet letters.

Like a number of other crafters in the community, Donna and John Baxter turned their hobby into a full time career. After retiring from farming the flat fields of Ohio, John moved with his artist wife Donna to set up their home and studio on Ogle Hills Road, slightly off the beaten path of the Great Smoky Arts & Crafts Community. He now helps Donna cut and assemble the beautiful beveled and stained glass pieces she creates on a long wooden table in the middle of the studio.

Donna cuts some magical creations in her kitchen as well. Heart shaped cookies made from her old fashioned **Sugar Cookies** recipe are a hit on Valentines Day; and her **Everything Cake** and **Pineapple Salad** are two must try recipes.

Sugar Cookies

Donna Baxter
Baxter's Stained Glass

This wonderful old-fashioned recipe was given to Donna many years ago by a 70 year old neighbor, who inherited it from her mother. The original measurements called for a "coffee cup full of." This recipe has been tested using standard measuring cups.

Donna makes these for Valentines Day. She cuts the dough with a large heart shaped cookie cutter and sprinkles them with red sugar. I found this recipe perfect for making Stack Cake. It makes 4 stacks plus enough dough for an additional 3 dozen cookies.

1 cup shortening	2 tablespoons hot water
2 cups sugar	⅛ teaspoon salt
2 eggs, plus milk to fill an 8-ounce cup	1 teaspoon baking soda
1 teaspoon vanilla (or lemon flavoring)	2 teaspoons baking powder
	5 cups flour

1. Cream together shortening and sugar. Add eggs, milk, vanilla, and hot water. Sift together salt, baking soda, baking powder, and flour. Stir into creamed mixture.

2. Preheat oven to 375°. Roll dough on floured board. Cut into shapes. Bake on greased cookie sheet for 12 minutes at 375°. Cool on racks.

Todd-Thomas Cookie Pizza

Pat K. Thomas
PEWTER BY HEDKO

At the Thomas house, everybody gets into the act when topping this pizza. Sprinkling their favorite toppings on evenly, artistically, randomly, and lavishly, the whole family shares in the fun. Pat says "We don't measure anything. We just sprinkle a lot on until it looks good, or use up what we have!"

"The hardest part of this recipe is greasing the foil (because it crinkles)" says Pat. Her advice is "Go slow and use as many hands as possible to keep the foil straight." I say, "Just bring out the can of non-stick cooking spray and give it a spritz. Then you can say 'Look Ma, no hands.'"

20 ounce package refrigerated sugar cookie dough	1 cup miniature marshmallows
½ cup chopped nuts	1 cup semi-sweet chocolate chips
	⅓ cup caramel ice cream topping

1. Preheat oven to 350°. Line a 12" pizza pan with foil. Grease with margarine or non-stick spray. Press cookie dough onto foil-lined pan.

2. Bake for 13 to 16 minutes, until light golden brown. Remove from oven. Sprinkle all the nuts, marshmallows, and chips on top. Drizzle with ice cream topping. Bake an additional 5 to 10 minutes until the marshmallows brown. Cool completely. Remove foil. Cut into pizza wedges to serve. Serves 8 to 10.

Variation: Ideas to add, substitute, or experiment with: butterscotch chips, raisins, dried cranberries, peanuts, pistachio nuts, pecans, cashews, refrigerated chocolate chip cookie dough.

Oatmeal Shortbread Squares

Wilma Prebor
QUILTS BY WILMA

These squares are crumbly, but good. A great treat for school lunches. In fact, why not let the kids make this simple recipe. They will like mixing it with their hands.

3 ½ cups oatmeal, not instant	⅔ cup sugar
¼ cup flour	¾ cup margarine, softened
½ teaspoon salt	1 teaspoon vanilla

1. Preheat oven to 350°. Generously grease and flour 8" x 8" baking pan. In a large bowl combine oatmeal, flour, salt, sugar, margarine, and vanilla. Mix together well with hands. Press into prepared baking pan. Bake for 30 minutes. Cool for 15 minutes before cutting into squares.

"Grandma's Quilt"

My wedding present from Grandma was a wool quilt made from the hand-woven garments my great grandparents brought with them from Germany. While pregnant with my son, I was in bed for four months with it over me. The kids put it over chairs to make a playhouse when it was raining. While my son was ill for three years before he died, he adopted the quilt. It got worn to a point where it was in shreds.

After he died, I took it off his bed and put it in a trunk. I thought "Golly, if I had realized the value of this quilt, I never would have let it get worn out like this." But then it was just like my late Grandma whopped me across the head and I said out loud, "No, this quilt was used just exactly as Grandma would have wanted it used."

I took it out several times to try and find an area in the quilt that would be good enough to make a wall hanging, but there just wasn't. After 10 years I think somebody "whopped" me again. I got a bright idea. I pieced together a teddy bear with salvaged fabric from Grandma's quilt. That experience helped me to understand what went into a quilt and what you can receive from a quilt.

—Wilma Prebor
Quilts by Wilma

Pewter by Hedko the Metal Spinner

*I*n a unique, one-of-a-kind, shop in Gatlinburg, John Thomas spins pewter into elegantly simple designs. Each piece a signed original, John refers to his works as "Heirlooms of Tomorrow." He uses only the finest pewter alloy in his craft, as established by his uncle and aunt, Helmut and Doris Koechert back in 1969.

"People come from all over the world to my shop." John says, "The story behind their desire to come here is as interesting as the visitors themselves." He is often intrigued by how collectors discover his shop. Once, within months after a free-lance writer wrote about him in the Los Angeles Times, he had 12 people arrive at his studio specifically because of the article. Ten of them had the article in their hand to be certain they found his shop!

John's wife, Pat, is an artist. Her marbled watercolor papers and calligraphy decorate the walls of the shop. Both John and Pat have contributed some wonderfully creative and scrumptious recipes to this book. John's **Summer Brownies** and Pat's **Todd Thomas Cookie Pizza** are not to be missed!

Summer Brownies

John Thomas
PEWTER BY HEDKO

This is John's own original recipe. He says, "Nobody else would actually consider combining these ingredients!" Well, John, they laughed at Van Gogh and thought he was crazy; but, in fact, he was a creative genius. Your combination of flavors and textures in this recipe is truly inspirational.

John says the name of this recipe is from "the ancient knowledge in all humankind wherein, when it comes to brownies, some 'R' better than others!" His advice is, "better make two, the first one may not get out of the kitchen."

1 extra moist brownie mix
miniature marshmallows
1 banana, very thinly sliced
   (see notes)

6 ounces butterscotch chips
frozen whipped topping, defrosted
   (see notes)

1. Bake brownie mix as per package instructions, except remove from oven 5 minutes before they are done. Completely cover brownie with marshmallows.

2. Cover marshmallows with banana slices. Spread butterscotch chips evenly over banana layer. Return to oven for 5 to 10 minutes until top looks melted. Allow to cool.

3. Apply at least a ½" thick layer of whipped topping (the richer the better) over your brownie and refrigerate. Serves 1 to 25.

Notes: Slice banana immediately prior to laying them. You may slice brownie and serve each piece with topping. However, spreading the whole brownie with topping helps to preserve banana and, most importantly, make it nearly impossible to identify the flavors hiding within.

Wilma's Lemon Squares

Wilma Prebor
QUILTS BY WILMA

This makes an excellent square to have on hand for a snack, or to take to a school bake sale. The lemon glaze is just the right combination of tart and sweet.

Lemon squares

1 cup sifted flour
3 tablespoons sugar
⅓ cup butter
2 eggs, beaten
½ cup brown sugar

½ cup chopped nuts
¾ cup coconut
¼ teaspoon salt
¼ teaspoon baking powder
½ teaspoon vanilla

Lemon glaze

1 cup powdered sugar, sifted
2 teaspoons grated lemon rind

2 tablespoons lemon juice

1. Preheat oven to 350°. In a mixing bowl, combine flour and sugar. Cut in butter until like fine crumbs. Press into an ungreased 8" x 8" pan. Bake for 20 minutes.

2. In mixing bowl, combine eggs, brown sugar, nuts, coconut, salt, baking powder, and vanilla. Mix well. Pour on baked dough and bake again for 25 to 30 minutes. Frost with lemon glaze while still hot. Cool, slice, and serve.

3. To prepare lemon glaze: Whisk together powdered sugar, lemon rind, and lemon juice until smooth.

Chocolate Espresso Truffles

Kathy Shields Guttman

To end a meal with a simple elegant dessert, place these rich chocolate morsels on a lovely serving platter surrounded by fresh strawberries. Serve with freshly brewed hot coffee and, if desired, your favorite liqueur.

8 ounces semi-sweet chocolate
3 ½ tablespoons butter
2 teaspoons instant coffee powder

¼ cup evaporated milk
1 tablespoon cocoa
1 tablespoon powdered sugar

1. In a saucepan, or in microwave, melt together chocolate and butter. Beat until smooth. Add instant coffee powder and evaporated milk. Stir until smooth. Place in refrigerator until well chilled. Roll chilled mixture into 1" balls and chill again.

2. In a small bowl, combine cocoa and powdered sugar. Roll balls in mixture to coat. Return to refrigerator to chill until ready to serve.

Variation: You may eliminate cocoa and powdered sugar coating, and roll in crushed toasted hazelnuts.

Woods by Weiss

*A*fter farming for 25 years in Benton County, Indiana, Walt and Garnet Weiss decided to move to the Smokies and turn their hobbies into a full time career.

Walt does lathe work and carving, but his specialty is marquetry. He creates landscape and wildlife art with natural colors of inlaid veneer. To achieve the colors he wants without using dyes, he imports wood veneers from all over the world.

Garnet says she "has been sewing forever." She does needle art, such as appliqued sweatshirts, dolls, cross stitch, and other wearable items. Walk into their studio and Garnet is usually there sitting by the window working on one of her sewing projects, or behind the counter doing the more mundane, but necessary, task of accounting.

Garnet and Walt enjoy having friends in for "casual meals and good conversation." Garnet says she likes to make the "quickest thing that looks like I've spent some time doing it." Her recipe for **Chicken Stuffing Casserole** definitely fits into that category. It is quick, easy, and delicious. For dessert, make up a batch of her **Peanut Brittle**.

Peanut Brittle

Garnet Weiss
WOODS BY WEISS

I felt like a "mad scientist" while preparing this fun and easy treat. When adding baking soda to the mixture, it instantly began to foam, froth, expand, and change to a golden opaque color. Beware, however, this mixture becomes extremely hot and would not be appropriate for kids to make without adult supervision. This recipe may be cut in half.

2 cups sugar
1 cup light corn syrup
½ cup water
1 tablespoon butter

2 cups salted peanuts
1 teaspoon vanilla
3 teaspoons baking soda

1. Butter two cookie sheets and set aside. In a saucepan, mix sugar, corn syrup, and water. Over medium high heat, stirring constantly, bring mixture to a crack stage (approximately 260°). Add butter and peanuts. Lower heat to medium. Stir and cook until a light golden brown. Be careful not to burn peanuts.

2. Remove from stove and add vanilla. While slightly tilting pan, fold in baking soda (the mixture will foam and expand). Pour onto prepared cookie sheets. Tilt sheet to level mixture, do not use spoon to level. Cool completely then break into pieces. Store in airtight container.

To clean faucets in bathroom use toothpaste—they will shine!

—Garnet Weiss
Woods by Weiss

Nanna's Drop Fudge

Jane Malone

When Jane, a customer of Betty Jane Posey, heard about this cookbook, she mailed me this recipe. She warns you that "This requires 10 minutes of your undivided attention. Once it is boiling, and until you finish dropping it onto wax paper, do not leave the fudge, don't even answer the phone."

Do not let her warnings scare you. This fudge is easy to prepare. It has a wonderful hint of peanut butter flavor. My daughter likes to break up pieces and sprinkle them on top of ice cream.

⅔ cup evaporated milk
2 tablespoons cocoa
2 cups sugar
dash of salt

1 teaspoon vanilla
2 teaspoons butter
1 tablespoon peanut butter

1. In a medium saucepan, stirring frequently, cook milk, cocoa, sugar, and salt over medium heat. Once it comes to a boil, stir constantly, and continue to boil until it reaches the softball stage, about 220°. If you do not have a candy thermometer, test by dropping a small amount into cold water. When the fudge forms a ball, it is done.

2. Remove from heat. Add vanilla, butter, and peanut butter. Mix well. Drop by spoonfuls onto lightly buttered wax paper. Let cool and then remove. Store in an airtight container. May also be poured into a buttered dish and cut into pieces once cooled.

Appendix A

Address List of Participating Members of the Great Smoky Arts & Crafts Community

Below you will find an address list of members of the Great Smoky Arts & Crafts Community who have contributed recipes to this cookbook. If you would like to contact any of the members, you may write to them directly, or contact them by writing to the Great Smoky Arts & Crafts Community, P. O. Box 807, Gatlinburg, Tennessee 37738. By writing to this address, you may request an up-to-date map and guide brochure listing all the members and calendar of events.

The 1996 season opened with close to 80 members of the Great Smoky Arts & Crafts Community. Many of the original 28 charter members are still in business today. This growing community of artisans is not a stagnant group. From year to year new members join, some retire, some leave, and some change location within the community.

If you are planning a trip to the area, call Gatlinburg's Visitor and Convention Bureau at 1-800-568-4748 to order a Gatlinburg Vacation Guide. This helpful guide lists attractions, restaurants, shopping, and lodging information. The 800 number is staffed by many operators, but sometimes there is a long wait to talk to one of their "information specialists." It is best to call early in the day. If you have difficulty getting information on the 800 number, write to Visitors and Convention Bureau, 234 Airport Road, Gatlinburg, Tennessee 37738 to request a guide.

Nancy and Wes Hopf
ADOUGHABLE THINGS BY NANCY
623 Glades Road, Suite 15
Gatlinburg, Tennessee 37738

J. Alan
THE J. ALAN GALLERY
252 Buckhorn Road
Gatlinburg, Tennessee 37738

Robert Alewine
ALEWINE POTTERY
623 Glades Road
Gatlinburg, Tennessee 37738

Myriam and Ron Nolcken
ARTIST DOLLS BY MYRIAM/COBBLESTONES
1402 East Parkway, Suite 10
Gatlinburg, Tennessee 37738

Donna and John Baxter
BAXTER'S STAINED GLASS
1069 Ogle Hills Road
Gatlinburg, Tennessee 37738

Ed Byrnes
BYRNES WOODCRAFTERS
1402 East Parkway, Suite 5
Gatlinburg, Tennessee 37738

John and Connie Burns
BUCKHORN INN
2140 Tudor Mountain Road
Gatlinburg, Tennessee 37738

Jake and Lorraine Quilliams
BUCKHORN HANDCRAFTS
Retired

Buie Boling
BUIE POTTERY
1402 East Parkway, Suite 12
Gatlinburg, Tennessee 37738

Joan Royer
BUNNIES N BEARS BY JOAN
No longer members

Bill and Anita Cate
THE COLONEL'S LADY
1120 Taurac Trail
Gatlinburg, Tennessee 37738

Carl Fogliani
COSBY HILLPEOPLE CRAFTS
676 Glades Road, Suites 1 & 2
Gatlinburg, Tennessee 37738

Eugene and Sue Ownby
E & T WOODCARVINGS
459 Glades Road
Gatlinburg, Tennessee 37738

Karen Pierre
EARTHSPEAK
516 Buckhorn Road
Gatlinburg, Tennessee 37738

Frances Fox
FIBER CREATIONS INC.
678 Glades Road
Gatlinburg, Tennessee 37738

Jeff Hale
FUTURE RELICS
664 Glades Road
Gatlinburg, Tennessee 37738

Marsha Fountain
GATLIN COUNTY LEATHER
516 Buckhorn Road
Gatlinburg, Tennessee 37738

Mac and Susan McDonell
GEMSTONE
337 Glades Road, Suite 2
Gatlinburg, Tennessee 37738

Helen Vance
HELEN'S CORNSHUCK CRAFTS
Retired

Clarice Maples
HEMLOCK FALLS NIGHTLY RENTALS
629 Glades Road, Suite 2
Gatlinburg, Tennessee 37738

Gil Knier
HERITAGE ARTS CENTER
No longer member

Vern and Lisa Hippensteal
HIPPENSTEAL INN
P. O. Box 707
Grassy Branch Road
Gatlinburg, Tennessee 37738

Maria and John Holloway
HOLLOWAY'S COUNTRY HOME
465 Glades Road
Gatlinburg, Tennessee 37738

Victoria and Alan Aspurua
HOMESPUN HEART
No longer members

Al Shirley (Annetta Hendrickson)
LEATHER WORKS
P. O. Box 711
1402 East Parkway
Gatlinburg, Tennessee 37738

Gena and Mike Lewis
LEWIS FAMILY CRAFTS
601 Glades Road, Suite 13
Gatlinburg, Tennessee 37738

Alice and Jim Moore
ALICE MOORE GALLERY
680 Glades Road
Gatlinburg, Tennessee 37738

Marg Muller
MULLER GALLERY
601 Glades Road
Gatlinburg, Tennessee 37738

Becky Osteen and Martha Powers
OSTEEN & POWERS
1402 East Parkway, Suite 9
Gatlinburg, Tennessee 37738

John Thomas
PEWTER BY HEDKO THE METAL SPINNER
250 Buckhorn Road
Gatlinburg, Tennessee 37738

Betty Jane and Cecil Posey
BETTY JANE POSEY GALLERY
1402 East Parkway, Suite 11
Gatlinburg, Tennessee 37738

Otto Preske
OTTO PRESKE—ARTIST IN WOOD
535 Buckhorn Road
Gatlinburg, Tennessee 37738

Wilma Prebor
QUILTS BY WILMA
1662 East Parkway
Gatlinburg, Tennessee 37738

Dick and Margaret Seymour
SEYMOUR'S COUNTRY CRAFTS
No longer members

Eleanor Hopf
SHUCKS Y'ALL!
623 Glades Road, Suite 15
Gatlinburg, Tennessee 37738

David Bailey
TEAGUE MILL/CREEKSIDE RESTAURANT
155 Texas Lane
Gatlinburg, Tennessee 37738

Richard and Stephanie Lang
VILLAGE CANDLES
P. O. Box 456
1402 East Parkway
Gatlinburg, Tennessee 37738

G & Vickie Webb
G. WEBB GALLERY
Corner Glades/Buckhorn Road
Gatlinburg, Tennessee 37738

Charlotte Boles and Peggy Bailey
WHISPERING PINES WOODCRAFTS
No longer members

Cindy Black, Manager
THE WILD PLUM TEA ROOM
555 Buckhorn Road
Gatlinburg, Tennessee 37738

Walt and Garnet Weiss
WOODS BY WEISS
Retired

Ross Markley
THE WOODTURNER & BASKET SHOP
248 Buckhorn Road
Gatlinburg, Tennessee 37738

Jean and Darrell Moore
THE WOODWARE CO.
601 Glades Road, Suite 19
Gatlinburg, Tennessee 37738

 Great Smoky Arts & Crafts Community SINCE 1937

Appendix B

Address List of
Contributing Restaurants

I have listed below the names and locations of the restaurants in the area (some favorites of the members of the Great Smoky Arts & Crafts Community) that have kindly submitted recipes to this book.

John Burns
BUCKHORN INN
2140 Tudor Mountain Road
Gatlinburg, Tennessee 37738
(423) 436-4668

Joan McGill
GLADES DELI
801 Glades Road
Gatlinburg, Tennessee 37738
(423) 436-4595

David Hadden
THE GREENBRIER RESTAURANT
370 Newman Road
Gatlinburg, Tennessee 37738
(423) 436-6318

Dave and Anne Howard
THE SPICE PEAR
Morning Mist Plaza
601 Glades Road, Suite 21
Gatlinburg, Tennessee 37738
(423) 430-3866

Giacomo "Jock" Lijoi
CHEF JOCK'S TASTEBUDS CAFE
1198 Wears Valley Road
Sevierville, Tennessee 37865
(423) 428-9781

TEAGUE MILL RESTAURANT
Webb's Creek Holler
155 Texas Lane
Gatlinburg, Tennessee 37738
(423) 436-8869

Cindy Black
THE WILD PLUM TEA ROOM
555 Buckhorn Road
Gatlinburg, Tennessee 37738
(423) 436-3808

Index